ARTS&
CRAFTS
STYLE

ARTS&
CRAFTS
STYLE

ISABELLE ANSCOMBE

RIZZOLI
NEW YORK

First published in the United States of America in
1991 by Rizzoli International Publications, Inc.
300 Park Avenue South, New York, NY 10010

Library of Congress Cataloging-in-Publication Data
Anscombe, Isabelle.
    Arts & crafts style/Isabelle Anscombe.
        p.   cm.
    Includes bibliographical references and index.
    ISBN 0–8478–1328–2
    1. Arts and crafts movement—Great Britain.   2. Arts and crafts
movement—United States.   I. Title.   II. Title: Arts and crafts
style.
NK1142.A52   1991
    745.4′441—dc20   90–53578
                                                                        CIP

Printed and bound in Singapore

Frontispiece: Watercolour copy of an original
painting by Edward Burne-Jones's studio assistant, Thomas Mathews Rooke, of *The Dining
Room at The Grange* (Burne-Jones's house),
1904, furnished with a table by Philip Webb
made at the time of Burne-Jones's marriage in
1860, a Morris and Co. 'Sussex' chair, a painted
sideboard and two stained glass panels of min-
strel figures.

Part openers: Hand-printed wallpapers designed
by Archibald Knox.

Contents

Introduction

❧

'The devotees of this creed,' wrote the art critic and painter Roger Fry of the Arts and Crafts movement in 1926, 'cultivated the exotic and precious with all the energy and determination of a dominant class. With the admirable self-assurance which this position gave them they defied ribaldry and flouted common sense. They had the courage of their affectations; they openly admitted to being "intense".' The products of the Arts and Crafts movement were indeed deliberately and selfconsciously artistic – a vital expression of the individuality of the craftsmen and women who made them – yet, for many of its devotees (such as A. H. Mackmurdo, who saw the movement 'not as an aesthetic excursion; but as a mighty upheaval of man's spiritual nature'), it was far more than a mere style: it was a way of life.

The Arts and Crafts movement had its beginnings in the mid-Victorian reaction to the squalor, ugliness and inequalities caused by industrialization. It was a search, at times almost a sacred quest, for a supposed return to quiet beauty, simplicity and honesty, to 'olde English' hospitality and a sense of nationality, that found expression initially through a revival of the style and 'manners' of the medieval period, and then through the day-to-day experience of a craft workshop. As the young Pre-Raphaelite painter Edward Burne-Jones once said, it was a matter of venturing 'all on the unseen', as in some Arthurian romance.

Architecture and the decorative arts were seen as a reflection of the health of a society: no wonder, so the argument went, that a people who can tolerate furnishings and public buildings created out of a mishmash of half-understood past styles, using materials totally unsuited to their purposes, have to endure working-class agitation, riots and other such signs of misery and confusion. Many shared A. H. Mackmurdo's view on the relationship between industrialization and class relations: 'All interest and joy in the work having gone, the man's interest gravitates to his wage. These working men become known . . . not as individuals, but as a class . . . with somewhat disturbing results to the community.'

In the 1880s the designers who allied themselves to the Arts and Crafts movement set out to subvert the contemporary tendency to use art as a means of signifying grandeur and power, and to propagandize a visual democracy of humble, plain, honest furniture. What had once been considered minor household arts became the decorative arts, which, together with architecture,

Stained glass panel made by Morris and Co. after a design by Edward Burne-Jones, of a female figure representing Justice

Above: Silver kettle on a stand and a lidded cup designed by C.R. Ashbee for the Guild of Handicraft

now took their place beside painting and sculpture. Just as John Ruskin had perceived the work of the masons who carved the gargoyles and stonework of the medieval cathedrals to be an expression of their individual humanity, so the guildsmen of the Arts and Crafts movement saw craft practice as a celebration of the expressive potential that lay within even the most humble worker.

It was but a short step from self-expression to the recognition of the legitimate rights of the workers, and many designers followed William Morris along the path of socialism. In setting up the Guild of Handicraft, C. R. Ashbee's avowed aim was no less than 'the destruction of the commercial system, to discredit it, undermine it, overthrow it'. Followers of the Arts and Crafts movement passionately believed that the only way to quell working-class unrest was to create working conditions that would restore the worker's dignity and give him satisfaction in his labour. These conditions were

to be found by looking back to the medieval guild system which had existed in harmony with traditional, largely rural communities. The new socialist Utopia was to be established on the basis of the craft guild. As C. R. Ashbee wrote in 1908, even after the failure of his own Guild: 'Industrial machinery is now finding its limitation, and therefore a new political era is beginning.'

Although not all Arts and Crafts designers rejected the use of the machine, few believed in the Victorian doctrine of progress, of a future made increasingly perfect by technological advance. Within the workshop, the machine must not dictate to the craftsman, nor limit his expressive freedom: the true purpose of the craft workshop was, according to Gustav Stickley, 'not the work itself, so much as the making of the man; the soul-stuff of a man is the product of work, and it is good, indifferent or bad, as is his work.' This led some craftsmen to adopt an almost artificial crudeness in the style of their work, and some writers to adopt an

'Cromer Bird' printed cotton designed c.1884 by A.H. Mackmurdo and printed by Simpson and Godlee. Victoria & Albert Museum, London

anti-intellectual stance in their critical appreciation of Arts and Crafts products. As the American writer and architect Charles Fletcher Lummis put it: 'Any fool can write a book but it takes a man to dovetail a door.'

But the Arts and Crafts movement remained a middle-class revolution. It affected the taste and buying habits of middle-class consumers, who were taught to display their taste and sensibility by redecorating their houses with 'Art' furnishings. And, by making art respectable and even worthy, it allowed many young gentlemen to reject careers in law or banking in favour of architecture or workshop experience, and hundreds of ladies to earn money from their handiwork.

The movement was predominantly British; only in America was it directly copied, adapted and continued into parallel traditions. On the Continent, designers were inspired by the movement's ideals but did not necessarily follow its style. Indeed, there is no single recognizable style that was Arts and Crafts. An interior could be exotic and precious, with rich colours and patterns, or whimsical and self-consciously artistic, or downright plain and homely. Proportion, simplicity of form, fitness for purpose, honesty to materials, the revival of 'lost' craft techniques and the enhancement of natural textures are all elements which, added to hand-craftsmanship, combined to create the Arts and Crafts style. To the Victorian generation, brought up on cabriole legs, cut glass and ormolu decoration, however, such simple, honest furniture must have seemed daringly innovative; and the social aims of the movement, too, were almost frighteningly liberal.

Part One

COHERENCE OUT OF CHAOS

The Search for a New Style

The Great Exhibition – the world's first-ever international exhibition – was held in Joseph Paxton's Crystal Palace in Hyde Park, London, in 1851. There were thousands of exhibitors, and the event was an unabashed celebration of British wealth, power and know-how, designed as a showcase for the artistic prowess of a great imperial and industrial nation: 'a marvellous, stirring, bewildering sight – a mixture of a genii palace, and a mighty bazaar', thus Charlotte Brontë described her impressions. It made a vast profit, and successfully distracted the British people from the political and industrial unrest of the previous decade; yet not everyone agreed on its splendour. Edward Burne-Jones, for example, described the 'gigantic weariness' of the Crystal Palace, and John Ruskin saw it merely as 'a greenhouse larger than had ever been built before'.

Certainly, in their desire to outdo one another in luxury and ingenuity, manufacturers of furniture, ceramics, textiles and other decorative artefacts attained new heights of vulgarity, imitating every conceivable period and style, and often combining several in one object: the majority of exhibits were met with cries of outraged good taste.

Revivals of past styles had been popular since the beginning of the century – for example, Horace Walpole's Strawberry Hill Gothick, Sir Walter Scott's great hall at Abbotsford, Sir Charles Barry's Gothic designs for the Houses of Parliament or Anthony Salvin's Elizabethan revival houses – but these had usually tended to be carefree, with little attempt to puzzle out the original grammar of a period. Gradually, however, the spirit of the age was brought to bear on such levity, and greater knowledge and understanding were insisted upon.

In *The Grammar of Ornament*, published in 1856, Owen Jones, one of the critics of the Great Exhibition, attempted an overview of the principles that underlay different national and historical styles. The notion of principles of design caught the imagination of a public sold on the doctrine of progress based on discoverable scientific laws. Even the official Government Schools of Design were reformed according to these new ideas by Henry Cole, who had assisted Prince Albert in the organization of the 1851 Exhibition. Design, said Cole and his followers, was like science, and the job of designing a carpet or table-cloth well should be a matter merely of discovering the correct principles and applying them. In 1857 Cole established a new Museum of Manufactures,

The gallery overlooking the entrance hall at 8 Addison Road, Holland Park, London, designed by Halsey Ricardo in 1907 for Ernest Debenham

Frederic E. Church's
Moorish-style Court Hall at
'Olana', built in the 1880s
above the Hudson River,
New York State

renamed the Victoria and Albert Museum in 1899, to provide a study collection of both historical and approved contemporary artefacts for commercial designers.

As the century progressed, designers and manufacturers made greater efforts to be exact in their imitations. Owen Jones had popularized Moorish architecture in his *Plans, Elevations, Sections and Details of the Alhambra*, (1836-45), and his designs for furniture for Jackson and Graham, and for wallpapers, silks and carpets, were based on Renaissance or Moorish styles. In the 1870s in New York, cabinet-makers such as Anthony Roux or Kimbel and Cabus made Renaissance revival furniture, and the Renaissance revival style of the architectural firm McKim, Mead and White remained popular.

A desire for novelty or the exotic ensured that revivalism remained a potent force, especially in public rooms and buildings such as hotels. Louis Comfort Tiffany created rooms in the Moorish style; the slightly erotic classicism of Lawrence Alma-Tadema's paintings received popular acclaim; the 'archaeological' jewellery of Castellani or Carlo Giuliano created a new fashion; while the craze for Japonisme swept both America and Europe. Certain individuals were drawn to specific cultures: William Morris collected Islamic arts from Persia, Turkey and Spain, William de Morgan drew heavily on Persian originals in his ceramics, Christopher Dresser often employed Egyptian motifs in his furniture, while the Manx artist Archibald Knox led a revival of interest in Celtic forms.

Artists especially appreciated the bohemian aspect of romantic foreign cultures –

Frederic, Lord Leighton, created his Moorish hall in Holland Park in the 1860s, while in the 1870s the American painter Frederic E. Church built himself a Persian palace, named Olana, on a hilltop overlooking the Hudson River. Revivalism remained a vital element in architecture and design well into the twentieth century.

But while critics of design reacted to the lavish vulgarity of the Great Exhibition with demands that designers become more scholarly in their approach to historical sources, social critics insisted that they adopt one coherent, national style, to suit the age and, moreover, symbolically unify and heal a fragmented nation 'at once destitute of faith and terrified at scepticism', as Thomas Carlyle had written in 1836.

One suggestion for a fitting national style had already been forcefully put forward in the 1830s by a young draughtsman, still only in his mid-twenties, who had recently converted to Catholicism – Augustus Welby Northmore Pugin. The Catholic Emancipation of 1829 and the Oxford Movement of the 1830s had fostered interest in the ceremonial and ritual practices of pre-Reformation days and encouraged nostalgia for the Middle Ages. To Pugin, the medieval cathedral symbolized a sense of community lacking in modern times: 'Catholic England was merry England,' he wrote in 1841, 'at least for the humbler classes; and the architecture was in keeping with the faith and manners of the times – at once strong and hospitable.' In 1836 he published *Contrasts; or a Parallel between the Noble Edifices of the Middle Ages and the corresponding Buildings of the Present Day: showing the Present Decay of Taste*, a frankly

Illustration from A.W.N. Pugin's *Contrasts*, 1836, showing the 'Present Decay in Taste'

2

c   b   a

1

3

propagandist pamphlet which advocated Gothic as the most apt symbol of both national and spiritual cohesion.

In the flurry of articles which appeared in the wake of the Great Exhibition, Gothic emerged as the front-runner for a national style. It was now also championed by a Protestant, John Ruskin, who saw Gothic as expressive of the craftsman's freedom within an earlier benign, but now lost, social order; its regeneration would restore social harmony in a country riddled with class conflict. His influential books, *The Seven Lamps of Architecture* (1849) and *The Stones of Venice* (1851 and 1853), described how moral regeneration was to be brought about through craftsmanship, which he saw as a form of labour based on nature not the machine. Not surprisingly, he and others, including such redoubtable figures as Charles Dickens, exploded in anger at the principles of design put forward by Henry Cole or Owen Jones, seeing them as allied to those very products of science – the mills and factories – that had produced social unrest.

The most important of Cole and Jones's principles was conventionalization, and its greatest champion was the botanist-turned-designer, Dr Christopher Dresser. His motto was 'Knowledge is Power', and he believed that the more knowledge – whether of botany or historical sources – a designer brought to his work, the more truthful, and therefore uplifting, the finished design would be. At only twenty-two, he had contributed a plate to Owen Jones's *Grammar of Ornament* showing 'several varieties of flowers, in plan and elevation, from which it will be seen that the basis of all form is geometry'. He lectured in the Schools of Design, teaching that conventionalized design should be based on the underlying geometry of strict botanical truth.

But Ruskin passionately denied that such a regimented set of rules could ever be mistaken for art. Conventionalization, he said, cut the designer or craftsman off from 'natural delight' and that all-important freedom of expression which Ruskin found most potently in the medieval cathedrals. 'In all things that live there are certain irregularities and deficiencies which are not only signs of life, but sources of beauty,' he wrote in 1853 in his famous essay on *The Nature of Gothic*. 'No human face is exactly the same in its lines on each side, no leaf perfect in its lines, no branch in its symmetry. All admit irregularity as they imply change; and to banish imperfection is to destroy perfection, to check exertion, to paralyze vitality.'

In many key respects, such as an acceptance of two-dimensional pattern or the absence of applied, non-structural ornament, the end-products created by the followers of conventionalization differed little from work later produced by the Arts and Crafts designers who took Pugin and Ruskin's oratory to heart. But the principles championed by Cole, Jones or Dresser were anathema to Morris and his followers. Conventionalization supported the belief in scientific progress, which was also used to vindicate the economic doctrine of *laissez-faire* that had led to unrestrained industrialization, squalor and working-class unrest – the very ills that the adoption of Gothic as a national style had set out to defeat. With the writings of Pugin and Ruskin, revivalism became no longer simply a matter of style, but a burning question of moral regeneration.

Drawing by John Ruskin from his book *The Seven Lamps of Architecture*, published in 1849

The Choice of Gothic

The Gothic Revival swiftly took hold of the popular imagination, fuelled not only by the writings of Pugin and Ruskin, but also by the stirring tales of chivalry recounted by Sir Walter Scott in novels such as *Ivanhoe* or *Redgauntlet*, by the publicity given to the Eglinton Tournament of 1839 (an aristocratic re-enactment of jousting), and by the romantic images of the Pre-Raphaelites who painted Tennysonian heroines and Arthurian knights with gem-like intensity. Indeed, the notion of the creation of a contemporary Camelot remained current until the First World War, with medieval chivalry being allied first to a concern for the poor and oppressed, then, more poignantly, to an officer's responsibility for his men in the trenches. Philanthropy of this nature, allied to Ruskin's argument that it was vital for society that workers should be craftsmen, finding self-expression in their daily toil, and ultimately linked by Morris to socialism, became a central facet of the Arts and Crafts movement: good design should benefit both those who made an object and those who used it.

For Pugin, the Gothic Revival meant literally that – the accurate re-creation of a medieval England infused with the awe-inspiring mysteries of early religious practice. The interest of Catholics such as he in medieval ceremony and ritual led to a demand for furniture and equipment such as chalices, monstrances, pastoral staffs, crosses and candlesticks to replace those lost during the Reformation, and Pugin set about reviving 'lost' craft techniques for ecclesiastical metalwork, stained glass, tiles and embroidery. He had in fact made his first designs for metalwork when he was only fifteen; his earliest designs for furniture, working-drawings for Gothic furniture for Windsor Castle, had been made for his father, Augustus Charles Pugin, an architectural draughtsman. These first efforts were based on his father's work in the Regency Gothic style, and were largely fanciful, but, after a study of medieval originals, his ideas became radically more simple, following as closely as possible the structure and grammar of the original style.

In 1837, two years after his conversion to Catholicism, the twenty-five-year-old Pugin received his first major architectural commission, the remodelling of Scarisbrick Hall in Lancashire as 'a standing illustration of good old English hospitality', for the wealthy landowner, Charles Scarisbrick. Pugin, himself a great collector of antiquities, also furnished the house with 'ancient'

The Royal Gallery in the Palace of Westminster, London, with interior decoration and furnishings by A.W.N. Pugin

furniture and carvings which he imported from Europe. Like many of his major commissions, including Alton Towers, Staffordshire, and Abney Hall, Cheshire, that for Scarisbrick Hall came from a Catholic patron. But his most famous work was for the Palace of Westminster, rebuilt by Sir Charles Barry after the fire of 1834. Pugin had first been commissioned by Barry in 1836 to execute his drawings for the competition to rebuild the Palace, and later to make estimate drawings. By June 1844, when Barry employed him to design the interiors, Pugin was acknowledged as the foremost expert in Gothic.

A recent inventory of his surviving furniture in the House of Lords has revealed Pugin's astonishing creativity. Between 1844 and his death in 1852, he designed over one thousand pieces, including forty-nine different types of armchair and one hundred different tables. Many of the differences between pieces were intended to signify rank and dignity, a vital element in Pugin's medieval world. He believed that all decoration should be meaningful, and further, that 'all ornament should consist of enrichment of the essential construction'. He also held that nature should provide the basis of ornament, but rejected Ruskin's naturalism in favour of an architectural interpretation of structure. In his furniture designs, made by Gillow's of Lancaster and J. G. Crace and Son, Pugin relied upon the strong outlines of revealed construction, such as curved cross braces, enhanced simply by chamfered decoration, revealed tenons or geometric inlays.

After a period of insanity, possibly brought on by overwork, Pugin died aged forty in 1852. He had worked without assistants, and had produced nine major books and endless sketches of medieval buildings, as well as thousands of drawings for furniture, mouldings, brass door furniture, fireplaces, stained glass, tiles, curtains, jewellery, even inkpots. The richness and vision of Pugin's designs, allied to his belief that society itself would be healed by such architecture and interiors, cemented Gothic powerfully in the popular imagination, and many younger architects emulated the visual coherence of his style and were influenced by his ideas on the relationship between nature, religious symbolism and aesthetics.

In the mid-nineteenth century there were no full-time schools of architecture, and pupils learnt from their masters and by studying historical models. Gothic was now interpreted in a variety of ways, from Alfred Waterhouse's 'municipal palaces', such as Manchester Town Hall or the Natural History Museum in South Kensington, to the Venetian Gothic of Sir George Gilbert Scott's St Pancras Station; from William Butterfield's stately church furnishings to the more eclectic church silver and metalwork of Henry Wilson and John Paul Cooper at the turn of the century.

The writings of the celebrated French architectural historian, Eugène Viollet-le-Duc, who had been responsible for the restoration of several important sites in France, including Notre Dame in Paris and the ramparts of Carcassonne, regenerated interest in medieval French architecture. Like Ruskin and Pugin, he believed that design began with interior spaces, not exterior style. In 1853 Ruskin wrote in *The*

The Natural History Museum in South Kensington by Alfred Waterhouse, built between 1873 and 1881

Nature of Gothic: 'It is one of the chief virtues of Gothic builders, that they never suffered ideas of outside symmetries and consistencies to interfere with the real use and value of what they did. If they wanted a window, they opened one; a room, they added one; a buttress, they built one; utterly regardless of any established conventionalities of external appearance. . . .'

For architects such as Philip Webb or Frank Lloyd Wright, this teaching, allied to a belief in the primacy of nature as a source for ornament, supplied the basis of their 'organic' style of building; for Hector Guimard and Emile Gallé in France or Victor Horta in Belgium, this interpretation of Gothic directly inspired Art Nouveau.

But in the 1850s and 1860s perhaps the most important offshoot of the Gothic Revival was the regeneration of medieval craft techniques, which thrived as the study of medieval originals became more detailed and scholarly. With the development of the Arts and Crafts movement, this revival of traditional methods was allied to the Ruskinian ideal of a craftsman's way of life, that of living simply, close to the land, and in harmony with the raw materials of his trade, far from industrial machinery or the artificial bustle of the city. It began, however, in the desire to re-create the lost richness and beauty of the ancient cathedrals.

In 1837 Pugin had persuaded John Hardman, a fellow Catholic who ran his family's button-making business in Birmingham, to set up a firm of church furnishers and 'Medieval Metalworkers' producing jewellery, ecclesiastical metalwork, stained glass, embroidery and also painted decoration to Pugin's designs. With Hardman, Pugin pioneered the rediscovery of the medieval methods employed in making ecclesiastical stained glass. With another friend, Herbert Minton, he also contributed to the revival of the Cistercian technique of making encaustic floor tiles; from 1840 thousands of tiles, based on medieval originals, were made to Pugin's designs by Minton and Co. of Stoke-on-Trent and used in churches, country houses, town halls and other public buildings.

The man most closely associated with the revival of ecclesiastical embroidery was the architect George Edmund Street. Street had trained in the office of Gilbert Scott, and was associated with the powerful Anglican Ecclesiological Society. He became Professor of Architecture at the Royal Academy, and many influential architects trained in his office, including J. D. Sedding, Philip Webb and Richard Norman Shaw. Street's early embroidery designs for altar frontals, sedilia hangings, copes and other vestments used appliquéd motifs, including monograms, crosses and floral designs copied from fifteenth-century models and were executed by Jones and Willis of Birmingham. When exhibited in 1851 they received much attention and were often imitated. William Morris and Philip Webb, whom Morris met during the nine months he spent in Street's office in 1856, both became embroidery enthusiasts. In the mid-1850s Street's sister was a founding member of the Ladies' Ecclesiastical Embroidery Society, which undertook many of her brother's commissions, as did the Leek Embroidery Society, founded in 1879 by Elizabeth Wardle, the wife of

Oak cabinet designed by J.P. Seddon for Morris and Co., 1861, inlaid with various woods and painted by Ford Madox Brown, Edward Burne-Jones, William Morris and Dante Gabriel Rossetti with scenes based on the honeymoon of King René of Anjou. Victoria & Albert Museum, London

Oak table designed by Philip Webb, *c.*1868, for Major Gillum, one of Webb's earliest patrons, showing the influence of Japanese furniture

depicted in their paintings, and their interest in medieval furnishings led directly to the foundation of Morris, Marshall, Faulkner and Co. at 8 Red Lion Square in April 1861 (the firm was renamed Morris and Co. in 1875 when it was reorganized with Morris as sole proprietor). Several of their early pieces of painted furniture were exhibited in 1862 at the 'Medieval Court' laid out by William Burges for the Ecclesiological Society at the International Exhibition at South Kensington.

There had been a Medieval Court at the 1851 Exhibition, almost exclusively designed by Pugin and executed by Hardman's. In 1862, however, furniture by many different architects and painters was included. Burges himself showed six pieces; there were many examples of church furnishings by G. E. Street and others, Norman Shaw contributed a carved and painted bookcase, and J. P. Seddon exhibited an inlaid roll-top desk and the 'King René's Honeymoon' cabinet, with panels painted by Dante Gabriel Rossetti, Ford Madox Brown, Burne-Jones and Morris after Walter Scott's account of the honeymoon of King René of Anjou.

Morris, Marshall, Faulkner and Co., exhibiting for the first time, showed a variety of pieces of furniture, designed by Philip Webb, Rossetti and Madox Brown and decorated by Burne-Jones, Rossetti, Madox Brown and Morris, as well as embroidery, tiles and metalwork. The firm's contribution won them two gold medals and was commended by the jury for the 'exactness of the imitation' of the medieval manner. Seven stained-glass panels designed by Rossetti to illustrate 'The Parable of the

William Morris's associate Thomas Wardle, who owned silk mills at Leek in Staffordshire. Wardle, who had helped Morris with his early experiments in dyeing, also printed silks and cottons especially for embroidery.

In 1872, when the Royal School of Art Needlework was founded in London, the revival of embroidery as an art, not just a ladylike pastime, was complete. Many leading Arts and Crafts designers – Edward Burne-Jones, William Morris, Walter Crane, Selwyn Image – supplied embroidery designs for a wide variety of domestic purposes to be worked by the ladies associated with the School, and the high standards of their work, which was exhibited in Europe and America, inspired many followers.

The painted furniture and interiors of the Middle Ages were also revived, although often fancifully. The Pre-Raphaelite painters, for instance, were tempted to construct the romantic painted chests and cabinets

Vineyard' and made by James Powell and Sons of Whitefriars caught the attention of the ecclesiastical architect George Frederick Bodley, and led to the firm's most important early commissions.

Bodley, like Street, was a pupil of Gilbert Scott, and also a friend of Philip Webb. He belonged to the new generation that believed an architect should be concerned with every detail of a building, providing a complete scheme of decoration. Bodley in particular used painted decoration for interior walls and roofs, employing bright primary colours to add richness and harmony: '. . . imbue your building to your utmost with refined beauty and restrained power,' he said in an address to the students of the Royal Academy in 1885. 'Little and infrequent touches of beauty, if they must be few, grafted, as it were, on to a well-proportioned fabric, will give a building a tender grace, and it will be a delight to all passers-by. Be not afraid of beauty and richness when you can get it.'

Morris, Marshall, Faulkner and Co. were only too happy to provide such touches of beauty and richness. One of the firm's earliest commissions was from Bodley for a tiled fireplace in the hall of Queens' College, Cambridge, which Bodley was restoring, and two other commissions from Cambridge followed: stained glass for All Saints' Church in Jesus Lane and painted ceiling decoration for Jesus College Chapel.

In the 1860s Morris's firm was probably best known for its ecclesiastical stained glass, and supplied windows for many of the churches Bodley was building or restoring. Rossetti and the young and inexperienced Burne-Jones had first been introduced to

Powell's in 1857 as designers of cartoons for stained glass by Charles Winston, a lawyer and amateur archaeologist, who, with William Warrington, had published *An Inquiry into the Difference of Style observable in Ancient Glass Paintings, especially in England: with Hints on Glass Painting* in 1847. Winston was an adviser to Powell's, and had experimented with them in re-creating the original, rough and uneven medieval 'pot metal' glass. Morris and his colleagues continued to research traditional methods with glass supplied by Powell's, using strong colours and simple construction. Initially Rossetti, Burne-Jones, Madox Brown and Morris all designed cartoons for windows, with Morris in charge of colouring and Webb responsible for their arrangement. In the 1870s, when Burne-Jones took over sole charge of the firm's glass design, they began to produce domestic, secular designs, often based on tales from Chaucer or Malory.

Bodley later broke completely with Morris and Co. after the Society for the Protection of Ancient Buildings (known as 'Anti-Scrape'), of which Morris and Webb were founding members, criticized some of his church restorations. However, he had already established his own 'Art' decorating firm, Watts and Co. in Baker Street, in 1874, with fellow architects Thomas Garner and G. G. Scott, junior, to produce wallpapers, embroidery and church silver.

By the late 1870s Morris and Co.'s commercial success had come to rest mainly on the wallpapers and textiles designed by Morris himself, and the earlier, Gothic mood of their productions was dissipated in the light mists of the Queen Anne revival. Nevertheless, both Morris and Webb's ideas

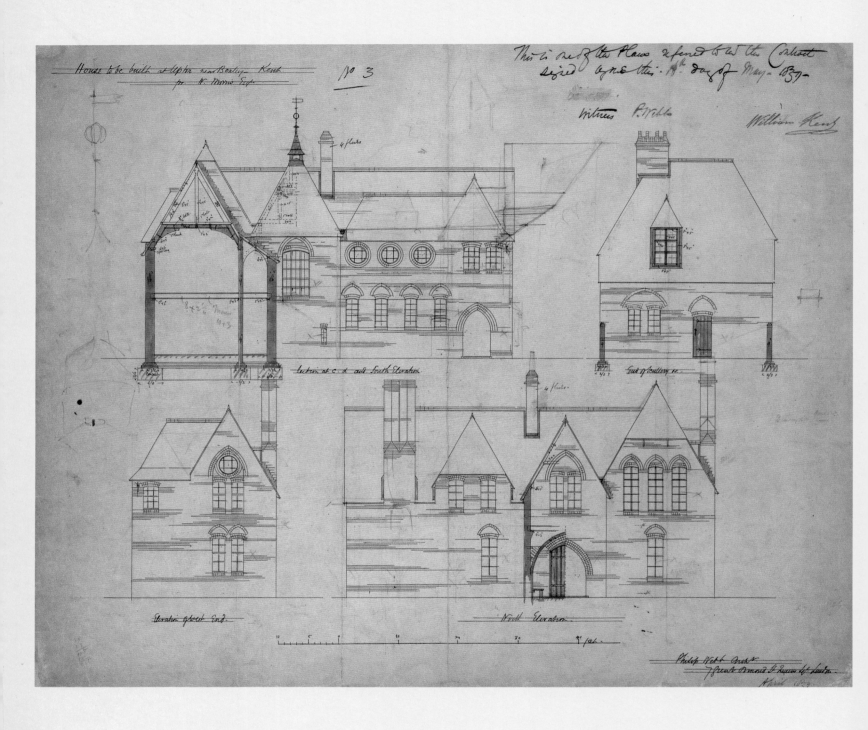

about interiors and furniture had their beginnings in the romantic medieval dreams of their youth, and especially in Morris and Burne-Jones's youthful veneration for Malory's *Morte d'Arthur* – on which Morris's first book, *The Defence of Guenevere*, and his paintings in the Oxford Union, had been based. Morris and Webb's journeys in France together in the late 1850s, when they had visited French cathedrals and especially admired the great French tapestries, had inspired the ideas put into practice in the Red House, built by Webb for Morris's marriage in 1859. As Lewis F. Day later wrote of Morris: 'he did all he could to forget six centuries or so and make believe we were living in the Middle Ages – a feat impossible for most of us, but all of a piece with the childlike simple-mindedness of the man.'

Webb believed that architecture should be both 'barbaric' and 'commonplace', possessed of rude strength yet not over-artistic. Morris, too, in his ideas for furniture, appreciated both grandeur and simplicity, and later wrote, in a lecture entitled 'The Lesser Arts of Life', that there should be both 'work-a-day' tables and chairs and 'what I should call state furniture ... sideboards, cabinets and the like, which we have quite as much for beauty's sake as for use: we need not spare ornament on these, but may make them as elegant and as elaborate as we can with carving, inlaying or painting; these are the blossoms of the art of furniture.' After his first, early experiments with painted furniture, Morris left Webb in charge of the firm's furniture production, but Webb's early designs, in their simplicity and proportion, show a sophisticated understand-

Bedroom suite in American black walnut with bird's eye maple veneer, by Daniel Pabst of Philadelphia, c.1875. Philadelphia Museum of Art

ing of the essential qualities of Gothic as first demonstrated by Pugin.

By the end of the 1860s the Gothic Revival, in both architecture and design, was being gradually absorbed into a less frankly imitative idiom of greater elegance and coherence, and some of the original emotional content of medieval romance was lost. In the designs of Bruce Talbert, for example, the revealed construction, the use of plain, unstained oak, and the added enrichment of mouldings and inset panels of the Gothic style were combined with the simplicity of strong horizontal and vertical forms and flat, naturalistic designs favoured by the new Anglo-Japanese taste of the early 1870s. Talbert, regarded in the 1860s as a leader in the field, designed textiles, carpets, metalwork, tapestries and wallpapers, as well as furniture for such firms as Jackson and Graham, Gillow's of Lancaster, J. G.

Opposite: One of Philip Webb's plans for the Red House, built for William Morris at Upton near Bexley Heath, Kent in 1859–60. Victoria & Albert Museum, London

books, *Gothic Forms Applied to Furniture, Metal Work and Decoration for Domestic Purposes* in 1868, and *Examples of Ancient & Modern Furniture, Metalwork, Tapestries, Decoration & Etc.* in 1876. These books helped to export this new, modern form of Gothic to America, where it proved to be enormously popular. The prestigious New York cabinet-makers, Kimbel and Cabus, for example, began to make pieces similar to those illustrated in Talbert's books, with elaborate metal strap-hinges and incised gilded decoration, carved panels or inset tiles, while still producing grand Renaissance-style furniture.

Although few Americans espoused the medieval ideal with the intensity of Pugin or the romance of Rossetti or Morris, there were many who admired Ruskin's writings and who adopted Gothic as a symbol of reform, in rejection of the over-lavish vulgarity of the mid-century. In Philadelphia, for example, the architect Frank Furness and the furniture designer with whom he collaborated, Daniel Pabst, were both influenced by Owen Jones's books and by Christopher Dresser, who lectured in the city in 1876, and Pabst began to make furniture of modern Gothic form. In Boston, the architect Ralph Adams Cram, a founder member of the Boston Society of Arts and Crafts, worked in the Gothic style, as did Isaac Scott in Chicago. Whatever the beliefs and ideals of individual men, however, there was no Gothic Revival in America; Gothic never became a movement, evincing the passions it had in England, but remained merely a style.

Further, as this more refined form of Gothic became popular in the mid-1870s in

Crace of London, Marsh and Jones of Leeds, and Lamb's of Manchester. Some of his later pieces were in mahogany or satinwood, or ebonized, with stencilled or incised and gilded decoration in the prevailing Aesthetic style, but his earlier, often massive, furniture made of fumed oak, with tongue and groove planking, relief carving or prominent metal hinges, created a smart new secular style of Gothic. The intensity of the Gothic Revival as a national mission thus ebbed away, only to be replaced in the 1880s by the more overtly socialist aims of the Arts and Crafts movement.

Talbert published two influential design

both England and America, it melded with the new vogue for ebonized furniture, which derived from the Anglo-Japanese taste of the Aesthetic movement. In England, a commercial firm such as Collinson and Lock, in their catalogue of 'Artistic Furniture' for 1871, illustrated pieces (possibly designed by the architect T. E. Collcutt), in both the modern Gothic style and in ebonized cherry with incised gilt decoration. The prolific designer Charles Bevan also designed for various commercial firms from about 1865, and in 1872 he set up his own company, C. Bevan and Son, Designers, Wood Carvers and Manufacturers of Art Furniture. He employed distinctive conventionalized designs, not unlike those published by Christopher Dresser, in dark-coloured inlays against lighter woods, as well as producing ebonized pieces.

In America, the greatest popularizer of secular Gothic was Charles Locke Eastlake, nephew of the Royal Academy painter. In 1872 his book, *Hints on Household Taste*, originally serialized in *The Queen* magazine in 1865–6, first appeared in Boston (and over the next decade there were seven American editions). Here Eastlake gave advice on the choice of tiles, curtains, door furniture and other furnishings, rejecting the false principles of naturalistic patterning or ornate carving in favour of the honesty of designs 'based on the sound artistic principles of early tradition', by which he meant Gothic. The illustrations of his own designs for furniture show side-tables and bookcases in the modern Gothic style which were eagerly copied in America and further popularized by the Philadelphia Centennial Exposition in 1876.

By 1870 furniture manufacture in America had moved away from the eastern seaboard to the river and railway towns of the Midwest, such as Cincinnati, Ohio or Grand Rapids, Michigan, where newly equipped factories, with native ash, cherry and walnut, could respond to the changes in taste led by Eastlake's book. Charles Tisch in New York, the Cincinnati firm of Mitchell and Rammelsburg, and, in Chicago, the Tobey Furniture Company, all produced furniture in the modern Gothic style during the 1870s and 1880s, although, in later editions of *Hints on Household Taste*, Eastlake was at pains to deny authorship of such furniture.

The accurate re-creation of the medieval world desired by Pugin or Ruskin had been side-stepped, but images of Arthurian legend or noble chivalry remained current well into the present century, demonstrating the power that the Gothic ideal held in popular imagination as a symbol of all that was worthy and true in British institutions. In America, while elements of Pugin or Talbert lingered on in 'reform' furniture, revealing Europe's continuing influence upon American taste, Gothic held a somewhat distant appeal, overlaid as it was by the more local call of Henry David Thoreau, Ralph Waldo Emerson or Walt Whitman and the equally romantic values of the wild frontier spirit. In a country that had so recently fought a bitter civil war, the notion of a mere 'national style' providing a social panacea was a little far-fetched. It was only in England, at once so anxious to deny social unrest and so fearful of it, that such a complex and subtle ideology as Arts and Crafts could develop and flourish.

Ecclesiastical window designed by Edward Burne-Jones for Morris and Co.

maria soror aaron

STAINED GLASS

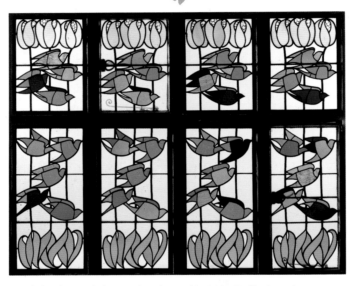

Leaded and stained glass window designed by M.H. Baillie Scott for a private
house in Douglas, Isle of Man and (*opposite*) a window designed by L. C. Tiffany

Stained glass underwent a revolution in the nineteenth century in both technique and design. Initially, firms such as Hardman's, Clayton and Bell, Heaton, Butler and Bayne or Lavers, Barraud and Westlake, and individual designers such as William Wailes, of Newcastle, and Charles Eamer Kempe, made painted glass in the Gothic Revival style for the hundreds of churches being built or restored in the 1850s and 1860s, but with Morris and Co. the idea of using clear glass with painted detail in paler tones as part of a scheme of interior decoration was introduced.

Designers such as Henry Holiday, who supplied to Powell's, Christopher Whall, who lectured on stained glass at the Central School of Arts and Crafts and pioneered the use of 'slab' glass, or Harry Clarke in Ireland, brought more painterly qualities to their figure painting, but leaded glass came gradually to rely more on colour and texture than on

painted decoration and, by the 1890s, was used not only in windows but also inset into doors and furniture.

In America, John La Farge and Louis Comfort Tiffany used layers of opalescent glass to create sumptuous, richly coloured windows with designs of flowers, exotic birds or shimmering skies which could not have been more different from the medieval-style windows made in England only thirty or forty years before.

M. H. Baillie Scott, Selwyn Image and Frank Brangwyn in England, E. A. Taylor and C. R. Mackintosh in Scotland, and Frank Lloyd Wright in America all designed leaded glass; in Europe, the Austrians Koloman Moser and Josef Hoffmann, the Belgian Victor Horta, the Frenchman Eugène Grasset and the Dutchman Jan Thorn Prikker also used coloured glass, generally with no painted detail whatsoever, or in strictly geometric designs, as part of their decorative schemes.

WILLIAM MORRIS

In his own lifetime William Morris (1834–96) was enormously influential: a busy, gregarious man, with wide-ranging interests, he was involved in many different causes, from the preservation of ancient buildings to revolutionary socialism. He is best known today for his textiles and wallpaper designs, but he also pioneered the revival of numerous techniques in crafts as diverse as the use of natural dyes and the design of typefaces, as well as being a prolific poet and writer, a tireless lecturer and a passionate Icelandic scholar.

He was born into a prosperous Walthamstow family in 1834 and educated at Marlborough and at Exeter College, Oxford. He intended at first to become a clergyman, but was already in love with the Middle Ages, through his avid reading of Sir Walter Scott and his wanderings among old churches, when he met Edward Burne-Jones and began to read Ruskin and Carlyle.

In 1856, following a trip to France with Burne-Jones when the two undergraduates decided to devote their lives to art, Morris entered the Oxford architectural office of G. E. Street, where he met Philip Webb. When Street moved to London later that year, Morris went too; he took rooms in Red Lion Square with Burne-Jones and they made their own heavy, painted furniture. Morris soon gave up architecture, and, inspired by a new friend, D. G. Rossetti, decided to become a painter.

It was in 1857, while they were working on the decorations for the Oxford Union based on Malory's *Morte d'Arthur* that Rossetti introduced Morris to a seventeen-year-old model he had discovered, Janey Burden, the daughter of a local stableman. She became Morris's 'glorious lady fair' and they were married in April 1859. They had two daughters, Jenny and May, but the relationship was not a happy one – she had a long affair with Rossetti – and this unaccustomed failure perplexed and saddened Morris throughout his life.

Edward Burne-Jones with William Morris at the Grange, Fulham, from an original photograph taken in the 1890s and (*opposite*) a page from an illuminated book of verse, *Lapse of the Year*, 1870, by William Morris

In 1877 Morris began his extensive programme of lectures on the decorative arts. He won over many young men to the cause of Arts and Crafts, and gradually came himself to see that the improvement of the decorative arts could not stop at romantic notions of re-creating the Middle Ages, but must lead on to real social change. In 1883, during his most prolific period as a designer, he became a socialist: he was a founding member of the Socialist League and first editor of *The Commonweal*.

In 1878 Morris had moved to a house overlooking the Thames at Hammersmith where, in 1890, he established his Kelmscott Press, the last great enterprise of his life.

THE LAPSE OF THE YEAR

SPRING am I, too soft of heart
Much to speak ere I depart:
Ask the summer-tide to prove
The abundance of my love

SUMMER looked for long am I
Much shall change or ere I die
Prithee take it not amiss
Though I weary thee with bliss!

Laden AUTUMN here I stand
Weak of heart and worn of hand;
Speak the word that sets me free
Nought but rest seems good to me

Ah, shall WINTER mend your case?
Set your teeth the wind to face,
Beat the snow down, tread the frost,
All is gained when all is lost.

MORRIS AND COMPANY

William Morris's drawing room at Hammersmith House in 1896,
showing various Morris and Co. products, including Morris's woven
'Bird' tapestry, pottery by William de Morgan, and an adjustable
armchair and a settle, both based on designs by Philip Webb

In addition to their ecclesiastical work, Morris, Marshall, Faulkner and Co. experimented with painted earthenware tiles, tapestries, embroideries, gesso decoration and wallpaper as well as furniture and stained glass during the 1860s, creating furnishings for medieval-style interiors. The work executed for such early commissions as the Green Dining-Room at the South Kensington Museum, the Armoury and Tapestry Rooms at St James's Palace or the interiors at 1 Palace Green, built in 1868–70 by Philip Webb for George Howard, later 9th Earl of Carlisle, was expensive but of very high quality.

Morris welcomed the artistic involvement of anyone associated with the firm: his wife Janey and her sister Elizabeth Burden both executed embroidery, as did Burne-Jones's wife Georgiana, while Kate and Lucy Faulkner, sisters of the firm's bookkeeper, Charles Faulkner, designed or executed tiles, gesso and china decoration, and wallpapers. Morris's friend William de Morgan, set up a kiln in the basement of his home in Fitzroy Square, producing tiles and stained glass for the firm. In 1872 he moved to Cheyne Row, Chelsea, where he 'rediscovered' the lost art of lustre decoration for pottery after observing accidental iridescence on stained glass. The rich 'moonlight' and 'sunset' effects of the copper, silver and gold lustres, and the gorgeous blues and turquoises of his Islamic-influenced 'Persian' wares (used for a wide range of tiles, bowls, chargers and vases) added a note of sumptuous luxury to the more subdued colours of Webb's early decorative schemes.

In 1877 a retail outlet was opened by Morris and Co. at 449 Oxford Street. Morris's own designs for wallpapers and textiles, including embroideries, tapestries, printed cottons, damasks, brocaded velvets, silks and wools, as well as machine-made carpets and hand-knotted 'Hammersmith' rugs, provided regular sales of repeat orders and gave the company financial security. But they also took in stock from outside sources – items such as light fittings by W. A. S. Benson, who also designed furniture for the firm, and metalwork by John Pearson, who had worked with C. R. Ashbee's Guild of Handicraft.

Morris had produced his first wallpaper design, 'Daisy', in 1862 and began his textile experiments in the 1870s. Influenced by his extensive collection and study of historic textiles, he realized that any improvement in design required a return to basic techniques. He first experimented with vegetable dyes at the firm's premises at 26 Queen Square; then, from 1875, with Thomas Wardle, brother of the firm's manager, he not only developed a durable alternative to the 'crude, livid and cheap' chemical aniline dyes produced from coal-tar that he found so hideous, but also experimented with discharge block-printing as an alternative to engraved roller-printing. Wardle dyed all Morris's silks and wools and printed his chintzes from 1876 until Merton Abbey, the site of a disused silk weaving shed on the river Wandle, only seven miles from London and ideal for workshops, was purchased by the firm in June 1881.

In 1890 George Jack, who had worked in Philip Webb's architectural office for ten years, took over as chief designer. He added a lightness and sophistication to the firm's style, which was evident in such later interiors as Clouds, Wiltshire, built by Webb for the Hon. Percy Wyndham, and Standen, Sussex, also built by Webb for a London solicitor, James Beale.

On William Morris's death in 1896, W. A. S. Benson took over the direction of the company, which continued to sell Morris chintzes, wallpapers, carpets and furniture until it went into voluntary liquidation in 1940.

Above: Design by William Morris for a wallpaper, in pencil and watercolour

Left: Interior of the Green Dining Room at the South Kensington Museum (now the Victoria & Albert Museum), decorated by Morris and Co. in 1866. Victoria & Albert Museum, London

The Victorian Fear of Chaos

While Gothic seemed to refer back to a lost golden age of craftsmanship and social harmony, it also excited a *frisson* of medieval fearfulness which very much appealed to the dark underside of nineteenth-century Britain. The Victorians were terrified of chaos, especially the chaos threatened by working-class unrest and agitation. Memories of the Luddites had not entirely faded, and the European revolutions of 1848, mirrored in Britain by the Chartist risings, seemed uncomfortably close. There was, too, in this age of science and education, a deep-rooted fear of all those newfangled, satanic mills: few people really understood just how such miracles of gas and steam actually worked, and many secretly felt that the progress they represented could somehow run amok, just as the workers – ignorant, brutish, fearsome – had threatened to do. And it was an ugly age. Life was full of dismal and brutal incidents: young children deformed by industrial accidents, famine in Ireland, cholera outbreaks due to bad sanitation, insanity caused by venereal diseases, and domestic drunkenness and violence. The truly grotesque was ever present. How better to disarm it than by a disowning laugh?

Charles Dickens used the grotesque as a literary style, employing distortion and exaggeration to provoke indignation and even revulsion over social evils, hypocrisy and greed, and his creations were immensely popular. The unpleasant characters in his novels were deformed, but had once been human, and so retained a point of contact with the reader, who must nervously and reluctantly have recognized something of himself in such debased creatures. The grotesque is distinguished by just this moment of recognition, and by that element of nervous humour which renders the familiar evil bearable.

Edward Lear's *Book of Nonsense*, published in 1846, and Lewis Carroll's *Alice's Adventures in Wonderland* (1865), followed six years later by *Alice Through the Looking Glass*, in which the *Punch* cartoonist John Tenniel's illustration of the Jabberwocky made its first appearance, all proved the popular appeal of the weird and distorted. The Jabberwocky, whatever its actual meaning for Carroll himself, remains a potent symbol of the Victorian fear of Darwinism gone wrong, of progress taking a wrong turn and allowing natural selection to evolve some hairless, clawed, two-headed, unimaginable creature. The rational principles taught in the Schools of Design were constantly shadowed by this

John Tenniel's illustration of 'The Jabberwocky' from Lewis Carroll's *Through the Looking Glass*, published in 1872

Illustration by Hablot K. Browne ('Phiz') depicting Mrs Sarah Gamp and a friend from Charles Dickens's novel *The Life and Adventures of Martin Chuzzlewit*, first published in 1843–4

subject-matter was tropical birds. William de Morgan, an admirer of Lear and Lewis Carroll, also developed an interest in grotesque forms of birds, animals and fishes while working at Merton Abbey in the 1880s, and J. Moyr Smith, who worked in Christopher Dresser's design studio, used a sometimes grotesque humour in his pseudo-medieval illustrations for tiles and Christmas cards.

But the ultimate in this combination of humour, caricature and outright unpleasantness were the birds, faces and nameless creatures created by Robert Wallace Martin and his brothers in Southall in the 1880s. The Martin brothers themselves were no strangers to the grotesque in real life, for their family was dogged by accidents and disasters. Their sister Olive was bitten by a monkey on her twenty-first birthday and subsequently died of the infected bite; Robert Wallace's daughter Amy had an illegitimate child, a sin which obsessed her over-religious father; a fire at their Brownlow Street premises in 1903 in which three people were asphyxiated so haunted Charles Martin, who managed the shop, that he eventually had to be confined to an asylum, where he died. Yet in 1882 one reviewer wrote of Robert Wallace's disturbingly vicious pieces: 'There is something so whimsically human in these fancies, they are so impossible and absurd yet so funny and attractive, that they remind us of nothing so much as the good old nursery rhymes. They are nonsense indeed, but good nonsense. . . .'

taste for the strange and grotesque which reflected a hidden current of fearfulness in Victorian society.

The most popular form of expression for this taste for the grotesque was the portrayal of animals and birds in realistic human situations. The architect and designer William Burges employed such devices on his painted furniture, often executed by Henry Stacy Marks, who worked as a muralist and decorator for him (and also for other architects such as E. W. Godwin and Alfred Waterhouse); Stacy Marks's own favourite

Another form of the grotesque echoed the ongoing debate about nature: was nature, as Ruskin upheld, beautiful only in

its divine imperfection, or did truth lie, as Christopher Dresser believed, in its underlying structure and geometry? The Ruskinian school culminated in the sinuous tendrils and exuberant curves of European Art Nouveau, but there were also artists who gloried in a more obvious distortion of natural forms. Christopher Dresser, for example, designed some tortured ceramic shapes for the Linthorpe Pottery, and echoed the twisted forms of Art Nouveau in his 'Clutha' glass. In America, the master of naturalistic distortion was the 'Mad Biloxi Potter', George E. Ohr. Ohr tended to portray himself as an untutored showman, a kind of circus act, but in fact had been apprenticed in 1875 to the ceramist Joseph

Meyer in New Orleans before returning to Biloxi, Mississippi, to set up his own pottery in 1893.

Ohr used local materials; the clay was thrown with superb skill to almost paper thinness, and then twisted, folded, pinched, dented and crushed into bizarre, ornate forms. This bravura was followed up with equal mastery of glaze techniques, and he often combined different mottled or speckled glazes, including metallic and crystalline effects, in a single piece. His claim was 'No Two Alike', and when he closed his pottery in 1906 there were several thousand pieces left in his warehouse. Contemporary critics did not know what to make of him, but he was undoubtedly unique.

Panel of tiles by William de Morgan

THE MARTIN BROTHERS

From left to right: Walter, Wallace and Edwin Martin in their Southall studio, 1912.
Opposite: two earthenware vases and a bowl, with various glazes, by George E. Ohr

The Martin Brothers – Robert Wallace, Charles, Walter and Edwin – founded their own pottery in 1873, moving from Fulham in 1877 to a disused soap factory on the banks of a canal in Southall. Walter was responsible for throwing and firing the salt-glazed stonewares, achieving a wide and subtle variety of blues, browns and greens; Edwin, who, like Walter had been apprenticed at Doulton's Art Pottery in Lambeth, did much of the painting and the raised and etched decoration of the vases and decorative pieces that they initially produced; Charles was manager of their Dickensian 'curiosity shop' in Brownlow Street, near Holborn; and the fiercely independent Robert Wallace produced the grotesque and strange sculptural pieces that were portrayed, even at the time, as quaint, old-fashioned and mysterious.

In the 1850s Robert Wallace had been assistant to one of the stone-carvers working on the vast building site of Sir Charles Barry's Palace of Westminster. In 1860 he enrolled in evening classes at Lambeth School of Art and the following year joined the studio of the sculptor Alexander Munro. The sly 'bird jars', as he called them, gaping spoon warmers and leering, two-faced Janus jugs which he produced during the 1880s prove him to have been a brilliant sculptor and an inspired caricaturist. By the late 1890s his creations had become pure sculptural fantasies, expressive of his obsessive sense of worldly sin and impending doom, for he was a fervent member of the fundamentalist sect, the Plymouth Brethren.

Collecting Martinware, and visiting the dusty Brownlow Street shop, full of its 'quaint grotesque creatures, hobgoblins, fish and uncanny beasts', fresh from the latest firing, became a kind of hobby for City bankers, lawyers and such patrons as the wealthy ironmonger, Frederick Nettlefold. Many of the 'bird jars' – ostensibly tobacco jars with detachable heads which could be moved to alter the creature's expression – are caricatures of barristers or judges, portraying a rogue's gallery of preening lasciviousness, disobliging spite and malicious hypocrisy.

By the First World War, when Robert Wallace finally ceased production, his three brothers had died. He himself died in 1923.

WILLIAM BURGES

'Ugly Burges who designs lovely things. Isn't he a duck!' wrote Lady Bute in her epitaph of the architect 'Billy' Burges, who died in 1881 while still in his mid-fifties. Burges, a bohemian, an enthusiastic Freemason, and a man with a taste for alcohol and opium, had many friends among the Pre-Raphaelites – Rossetti, Burne-Jones, Simeon Solomon, Henry Holiday and Edward Poynter all painted panels for his idiosyncratic Gothic furniture.

His principal patron was the 3rd Marquess of Bute, reputedly the richest man in the world, whom Burges first met in 1865 when the Marquess was only eighteen. Like Burges himself, Bute, a Catholic, was well-travelled, and an antiquarian with a passion for the Middle Ages. Burges, who collected medieval manuscripts, armour, embroideries, ivories, enamels, jades and gems, particularly admired early French architecture. As soon as Bute attained his majority, they began work rebuilding Cardiff Castle as a medieval treasury. Work was still unfinished when Burges died, but he had been closely involved with every detail of the castle, designing tiles, stained glass, carvings, painted decoration and furniture; even the basins for Lord Bute's bedroom were enhanced by Burges with monsters swimming about a stone arcade and a mermaid combing her hair, all in the style of Italian majolica.

In 1875 he began work on a second major commission for Bute, Castell Coch, and in 1878 moved into his own Tower House in Melbury Road, London – a daring make-believe castle with turrets and gargoyles on the outside, moons, mermaids and fairies painted in gold, silver and heraldic colours on the inside. It was the most complete expression of his private fantasies and provided an Aladdin's cave for his own collection. Each room was given a colourful theme connected with some legend, dream or joke. His bedroom was decorated with 'The Sea and its Inhabitants', while the library has an imposing chimneypiece showing 'The Dispersion of the Parts of Speech at the Time of the Tower of Babel', flanked by bookcases decorated with letters of the alphabet. The letter *H* is painted as having fallen

down from the cornice of the chimney-piece – a joke that Burges, in fact the son of a wealthy marine engineer, had 'dropped his aitches'.

Burges had a far greater understanding of the original medieval French models that inspired his painted furniture than had Morris and the Pre-Raphaelite painters, who merely added painted panels to a wooden carcass. Burges designed his furniture specifically for the decoration he had in mind, and linked the theme of the painting to the function of the piece – the letters of the alphabet in his library, for instance, Sleeping Beauty on a bed, mermaids in a bathroom or Narcissus on a washstand.

Burges was not only responsible for furniture and painted mural decoration; he also designed tiles, stained glass, mosaic, jewellery, and metalwork set with the antique coins, enamels, intaglio gems and semi-precious stones (lapis lazuli, jade, rock crystal) that he collected. A popular, gregarious man, he loved ceremony and enjoyed designing vessels or pieces of furniture for special uses; he was also very short-sighted, which perhaps accounts for the detailed, jewel-like appearance of his work.

Opposite: The drawing-room at Tower House, William Burges's Kensington house, photographed in 1885

Chest on a stand made by Burges for Tower House, 1875. Fred Weeks was probably the designer of the pseudo-medieval figures depicting Adam expelled from Paradise and reclothed, and of the images relating to male toiletry items.

Part Two

THE
EXPLORATION
OF
ARTS AND CRAFTS
IDEALS

A New Gospel is Spread

By the 1880s the popularity of Gothic as a decorative style had waned, but the ideals behind the Gothic Revival continued to be felt just as forcefully; as J. D. Sedding said in 1893, the Gothic Revival had been 'the health-giving spark'. The new movement (the term 'Arts and Crafts' was not commonly used until late in the decade) latched on to the ideal of a society regenerated by the values and skills of craftsmanship – an ideal espoused, in different ways, by Ruskin and Morris. The medieval craft workshop seemed to them to be clearly a more humane place than the modern factory or mill, and, further, they believed that the organization of labour, of masters and apprentices, within the workshop benefited the individual and provided a harmonious pattern for society as a whole. The consumer, freed from an environment of shoddy, machine-made imitations of unsuitably grand styles, would also be released into a world where his eye and mind would be rested and calmed by the presence of beautiful things made with love and pride.

The writings of Ruskin, and later Morris, were enormously influential not only in Britain but all over Europe and America, and during the last twenty years of the nineteenth century, craft guilds and artists' colonies inspired by their ideas were founded in many countries.

In 1871 Ruskin himself attempted to turn his beliefs to practical account, and founded the Guild of St George, but his somewhat paternalistic enterprise achieved little other than a small museum near Sheffield and some workmen's dwellings in Wales. In 1882, however, his friend and disciple, Arthur Heygate Mackmurdo, founded the Century Guild together with the designer and former curate Selwyn Image. Mackmurdo, an architect, had heard Ruskin lecture at Oxford, and in 1874 had travelled with him in Italy. A few years later, he had met William Morris and had become interested in the decorative arts. The Guild, which produced designs by Herbert P. Horne, Clement Heaton, Heywood Sumner and others, flourished for six years, and carried out decorative work of all kinds, including furniture, metalwork, textiles and wallpapers; everything was presented as a co-operative effort, though much was designed by Mackmurdo himself. His furniture was generally of mahogany and owed more to the eighteenth-century simplicity of the 'Queen Anne' style than to medieval Gothic; his flat designs were masterly, introducing a totally fresh, sinuous elegance into

Watercolour design by C.R. Ashbee for the dining-room of 37 Cheyne Walk, London, published in 1901 in *Kunst und Kunsthandwerk*, Vienna

53

pattern design, prefiguring the whiplash curves of Art Nouveau.

The success of the Century Guild inspired other like-minded designers to band together. In 1883 a group of young architects from Richard Norman Shaw's office set up the St George's Art Society to include 'craftsmen in architecture, painting, sculpture and the kindred arts'. Following in the footsteps of Shaw's own master, G. E. Street, who had encouraged his pupils to practise traditional crafts, they wanted a wider definition of the arts than the official line allowed by the Royal Academy or the Institute of British Architects.

In May 1884 the St George's Art Society joined forces with The Fifteen, a discussion group founded a year or two before under the secretaryship of the successful freelance designer, Lewis F. Day. (The Fifteen also included designers such as Walter Crane and Henry Holiday and the architect J. D. Sedding, another of Street's pupils.) The new society was named the Art Workers' Guild, and is still in existence today. It established common aims, provided a meeting place for discussion and a platform for lectures on techniques and styles; Morris, Norman Shaw, Mackmurdo, Ashbee, Voysey and Lutyens were among its many distinguished members (it did not admit women until 1964); all, despite their individual differences in style, swore allegiance to the Arts and Crafts movement.

The new idiom of Arts and Crafts was strong and simple in form, rich and intricate in craftsmanship, with a fresh morality based on fitness for purpose. While leaving Gothic motifs behind, the style had absorbed the architectural principles of furniture construction championed by Pugin, as well as the return to basics via the study of ancient, traditional techniques that (along with Street and Morris) he pioneered; Pugin and Bodley's love of colour and bold effect also continued unabated. These elements were combined in a new, eclectic style that stressed simplicity and an honesty of construction based on first-hand understanding of the materials employed, while encouraging richness, colour and the use of such precious materials as silver, enamel, mother-of-pearl or iridescent glass.

The architect and metalworker Henry Wilson, a master of the Art Workers' Guild, once described it as 'a club for artists', explaining that, 'as everybody knows, artists are unpractical cranks'. The pride that many of this first generation of Arts and Crafts designers took in being cranks – bohemian, anti-establishment, steeped in the lore of the studio or craft workshop – characterized the movement and the manner in which it presented itself for many years to come.

Arts and Crafts artefacts were honest, sturdy, and, by the standards of their day, decidedly eccentric, yet by the 1880s the style had established itself as the idiom of the liberal middle classes. A. H. Mackmurdo described his aim as being to make 'beautiful things for the homes of simple and gentle folk', which was just how those folk wished to see themselves. Although Morris and Co.'s early commissions had been for grand, indeed palatial, schemes of interior decoration, by the 1880s most Arts and Crafts designers had accepted Morris's own urgent desire to create not 'art for the few', but goods affordable by all. To some degree,

Morris and Co. had achieved this with their 'Sussex' chairs, upholstered armchairs and chintzes, but Morris wallpapers, for example, were always more expensive than most. However, as M. H. Baillie Scott pointed out in *The Studio* in 1897: 'The necessary restrictions imposed by a limited purse often prove to be the best safeguard against over-extravagance; and so to those who can appreciate the beauty of simplicity and restraint, necessity in this case may become a virtue indeed, and instead of trying to emulate the splendours of the palace, so often vulgar, so seldom comfortable and homely, we may accept gladly the limitations which suggest a more cottage-like home.' Simplicity, restraint and the supposed values of cottage life were indeed almost passionately adopted as virtues by those who rejected the ostentation of wealth derived from industrial muscle and from an unjust economic system.

In 1888 a splinter group from the Art Workers' Guild founded the Arts and Crafts Exhibition Society, which, until the First World War provided a showcase for both commercial and amateur designs. Walter Crane was its first president and Lewis F. Day its treasurer. Over five hundred objects selected by committee were shown at its first membership exhibition, held at the New Gallery, which had been set up in Regent Street by two former directors of the influential Grosvenor Gallery. To enhance the occasion, William Morris gave a demonstration of weaving to a selected audience and Isadora Duncan danced. From the start, the society's exhibitions included products from commercial firms, so long as both designer and executant were credited,

Mahogany settle with cane panels designed by A.H. Mackmurdo for the Century Guild, *c.*1886, with hangings and upholstery of Mackmurdo's 'Tulip' chintz, 1875

and in the 1890s retailers from all over Europe, including such notables as Samuel Bing from Paris, visited the triennial exhibitions in search of new talent.

The model provided by both the Art Workers' Guild and the Exhibition Society was quickly copied elsewhere: in 1897 the Boston Society of Arts and Crafts was founded, followed by similar organizations in Chicago, Detroit, New York and Minneapolis. For many, however, the new movement remained not simply a matter of style, but also a search for 'truth' and a solace for social ills. Thus A. H. Mackmurdo later wrote in his unpublished 'History of the Arts and Crafts Movement', it was important to '... see this movement not as an aesthetic excursion; but as a mighty upheaval of man's spiritual nature.'

The Arts and Crafts movement, which encompassed the notion that honest craftsmanship was good for both the craftsman and the inhabitant of a 'reformed' home, became increasingly allied to socialism. Many artists and designers, including Rossetti and Morris, had lectured at the Working Mens' Clubs in London's East End, and had seen for themselves the appalling conditions in which the poor lived and worked. 'Apart from my desire to produce beautiful things,' Morris later said, 'the leading passion of my life is hatred of modern civilisation.' If, as he fervently believed, the decorative arts were a standard against which the health of society could be measured, then his Ruskinian ideal of improving the decorative arts could not stop at romantic notions of re-creating the Middle Ages, but must lead on to real social change. For Morris, his cherished chivalric ideal that the strong should look after the weak developed into full-blooded political action, and in 1883 he became a socialist. The possibility of revolution was not remote. There had been working-class riots in London's West End in 1866 and again in February 1886, after a particularly severe winter, a meeting of the unemployed ended in rioting in Hyde Park and St James's. Morris, who spoke for the Socialist League at many open-air meetings at this time, thought these disturbances were indeed 'the first skirmish of the revolution'. He was not alone; several Arts and Crafts designers joined the socialist cause, including Philip Webb, W. R. Lethaby, C. R. Ashbee and, not least, Walter Crane, who painted pictures with socialist themes, designed union banners and contributed covers to *The Practical Socialist*.

But, as he outlined in his *News From Nowhere*, a description of life after the imagined revolution, Morris's socialist Utopia in fact harked back to a rural, medieval idyll based on craftsmanship. Support for this supposed remedy for social injustice came from Ruskin's absolute rejection of the machine, which he saw as having destroyed the vital irregularity and freedom of expression that symbolized man's closeness to nature. The machine had not only spawned the degradation of most factory conditions, but also created a false perfection which mirrored a vacuity within the society that consumed machine-made goods. Only hand-craftsmanship could be free, beautiful and creative. In much the same vein, C. R. Ashbee on a brief visit to Elverhoj, a Danish craft colony overlooking the Hudson River in New York State, wrote in 1915: 'The real thing is the life; and it doesn't matter so very much if their metalwork is second rate. Give them their liberty of production and they'll do it better.'

Ashbee had established his own democratic, profit-sharing Guild of Handicraft in the East End of London in 1888. By the end of the 1890s, when, the Guild became a limited company, it was doing very well, and Ashbee began to work towards his real dream, the establishment of his own Utopia, his 'city of the sun', a guild of craftsmen living and working in the countryside. In 1902 the Guild settled in Chipping Campden, and it survived for nearly five happy years before logistical and administrative difficulties got the better of it. As an experiment in true Arts and Crafts living, however, the Guild's brief rural retreat was of vital importance. Visitors came from all over the world, and the Guild's activities

'Cockatoo and Pomegranate', hand-printed wallpaper designed in 1899 by Walter Crane and manufactured by Jeffrey and Co.. Whitworth Art Gallery, Manchester

and products were much discussed and illustrated in magazines in Europe and America. In England, the Birmingham Guild of Handicraft, established in 1890, was closely modelled on Ashbee's Guild; in Munich, the Vereinigte Werkstätten für Kunst in Handwerk (meaning 'united workshops for art and craft') were founded in 1897; in Vienna, the Wiener Werkstätte was inspired by the Guild of Handicraft; and in 1901 Gustav Stickley in Syracuse, New York State, attempted a similar experiment in profit-sharing with United Crafts. However, none of these European or American guilds shared the largely British abhorrence of the machine, and, as a result, were successfully able to compete commercially in the market-place.

Nevertheless, after the failure of the Guild, Ashbee was more certain than ever that it was the way of life that counted, and that this could not include mechanization. In his book, *Craftsmanship in Competitive Industry*, he argued for legislation to protect craftsmen from industrial competition, and bitterly imagined the comment of the financier: 'If you cannot sell your things . . . your things are worth nothing, if you cannot sell your skill, your skill is worth nothing. . . . As for your workmen and their traditions, and their standard of life – that is not a question of practical finance and is no concern of mine.'

But the desire for a new way, for something better than the teeming squalor and degradation of the large industrial cities, for a style more modern and rational than the excesses of the mid-century, had caught hold. All over the world, art, architecture and design were discussed with as much passion as ecology and the environment are today. Art schools were revolutionized; in England, the Central School of Arts and Crafts was founded in London in 1896 with the architect W. R. Lethaby, a friend of Philip Webb's and a founder member of the St George's Art Society, as its first principal. Its teachers were drawn from the front ranks of the Arts and Crafts movement. In Birmingham, Liverpool and Glasgow, the art schools gave as much emphasis to ceramics, metalwork, furniture making or embroidery as to painting or sculpture; in Europe, too, the Secession movement called for architecture and the decorative arts to be given their proper place. In the 1880s a School of Applied Art was founded in Budapest and a journal of applied arts launched. Many new magazines were founded, using innovative printing techniques such as chromolithography. *The Studio* in England, *Pan, Jugend, Deutsche Kunst und Dekoration* and *Dekorative Kunst* in Germany, *Ver Sacrum* in Austria, *La Casa* in Italy, and *House Beautiful, House and Garden, Ladies' Home Journal* and *The Craftsman* in America all helped to spread the exciting new ideas about design and its connection with social well-being.

Perhaps the closest that anyone came to realizing Ruskin's personal and paternalistic vision was in Russia, where several craft colonies were established by aristocratic patrons to bring artist-designers and peasant craftsmen together. After Tzar Alexander II had freed the serfs in 1861, there had been renewed interest in the education and emancipation of the peasantry and in estate management. Among the liberal middle classes, there was also a fresh artistic awareness of Russian landscape and of traditional

Design for a carved and painted wooden cradle, with embroidered hanging, from the Talashkino workshops near Smolensk, 1906

Russian crafts, especially those associated with the Orthodox Church. Peasant culture, folklore, myth, and the colours, mosaics and icons of the Russian Church were adopted by many artists as the means of fusing together art, a sense of national identity and the spirituality of everyday life.

In 1875 the wealthy Moscow merchant, Savva Mamontov, and his wife Elizaveta founded an artists' colony at Abramtsevo, their estate near Moscow. Mamontov later also founded the Moscow Theatre, which inspired his cousin, Stanislavsky, to establish the Moscow Art Theatre in 1898. The artists associated with the Abramtsevo colony included the portraitist and landscape painter Valentin Serov, Mikhail Vroubel, who painted murals, undertook church restoration and made marvellous ceramics, and Vassily Polenov, who decorated the church at Abramtsevo. In 1885 the latter's sister, Elena Polenova, and her sister-in-law, Maria Yakunchikova, a cousin of Mamontov's, helped Elizaveta Mamontova to set up a wood-carving school to give the peasants a winter occupation. They introduced other crafts, including embroidery, painted decoration and, in 1890, ceramics. Yakunchikova, a painter who had made a study of the decorative motifs of peasant art and also collected fairy-tales and legends, later founded a carpet and dye factory on her own estate.

Polenova, formerly a student of drawing and ceramics in St Petersburg and an illustrator of Russian folk stories, ran the woodwork shop at Abramtsevo. She, too, founded her own workshops, the Trocadero, which produced furniture, pottery and embroidery and undertook bookbinding and illustration; she also accumulated an extensive collection of traditional Russian crafts. Her work inspired the foundation of another workshop in 1893 at Talashkino, near Smolensk, on the estate of the Princess Maria Tenisheva, a painter and a fine enamellist.

At Talashkino, the princess's retainers wore traditional white tunics and black boots; she revived interest in the balalaika; founded a school for peasant children where music, embroidery and design were taught; and established workshops where peasants produced richly carved and painted furniture, enamelwork, embroidery and ceramics which were sold in Moscow at a shop called Rodnik. Drawing on the folk traditions researched by Polenova, the Talashkino artefacts were decorated with stylized fish, flowers, birds and religious motifs.

In 1897 Princess Tenisheva met Sergei Diaghilev through Alexander Benois, whom she had employed to catalogue and organize an exhibition of her collections of folk art and Art Nouveau for her museum in Smolensk. Diaghilev visited her several times, hoping to obtain her financial support for the magazine he wished to start, *Mir Iskoustva* ('World of Art'). She and Mamontov both agreed to finance the periodical, and the first issue appeared in October 1898. It was highly influential and did much to introduce Art Nouveau to Russia and to promote Russian arts and crafts. One issue was devoted to the products of the Talashkino workshops, and in 1899 the second 'World of Art' exhibition featured embroidery designs by Polenova and pottery from Abramtsevo.

Elsewhere, young artists and architects in Europe were abandoning the fine arts to design furniture, textiles or metalwork. In Munich, the Secession was founded in 1892 by artists dissatisfied with the official Neo-classical style of the Bavarian government. It met with official disapproval, but for several years Munich became a centre of new ideas about design. The style set by designers such as Otto Eckmann, Hermann Obrist, Peter Behrens and August Endell, who among them designed furniture, light fittings, wallpapers, carpets, tapestries, embroideries, jewellery, ceramics, glass and woodcut illustrations, became known as *Jugendstil*, being named after *Jugend*, the innovative periodical founded in Munich in 1896 to which Eckmann contributed covers and illustrations

In 1897 Eckmann, Obrist, Behrens, Endell, Bernhard Pankok, Richard Riemerschmid, Bruno Paul and Paul Schultze-Naumburg broke away from the fine craftsmanship and self-conscious style of *Jugendstil* in order to design for industry. They founded the Vereinigte Werkstätten für Kunst in Handwerk, a community of craftsmen producing everyday objects with some common artistic unity. The name was derived from Morris's 'banded workshops' in *News From Nowhere*, but, although they shared the British aims of simplicity and fitness for purpose, the Germans did not support Morris's rural workshop ideal. The artists of the Vereinigte Werkstätten did not execute their own designs, which were made for them by skilled craftsmen using modern machinery. As a result, the Munich guild was commercially extremely successful. In 1902, in *Dekorative Kunst*, Hermann Muthesius described '. . . the peculiar

cultural image that William Morris and the English artist-socialists have given us of an "art of the people for the people" which, in the end, produced such expensive things that at the very most only the upper ten thousand could consider buying them.' Muthesius was a Prussian architect, civil servant and critic who had been attached to the German Embassy in London from 1896 to 1903. He had travelled all over Britain and in 1904 published *Das Englische Haus*, a book praising the architecture of the British Arts and Crafts movement and publicizing it in Europe, but at the same time casting a realistic eye over its Utopian dreams.

In 1899 the Vereinigte Werkstätten exhibited four rooms in Dresden at the *Deutsche Kunst-Ausstellung*. Their designs for furnishings showed a burgeoning awareness of the needs of serial, industrial production. As yet, there was no 'machine aesthetic'; the forms were curved, organic, unadorned and still based on methods of hand-craftsmanship, but the move towards the absolute refinement of form required by mass production was there.

In Vienna, the Secession, founded in 1897 in opposition to the established Academy painters with the painter Gustav Klimt as its first president, welcomed foreign inspiration and declared that 'We recognize no distinction between "high art" and "minor arts", between art for the rich and art for the poor. Art is public property.' It was the architects of the Secession, trained in the offices of Otto Wagner, who did most to champion the cause of Arts and Crafts. In his book *Moderne Architektur*, published in 1895, Wagner had provided the inspiration for the concept of the *Gesamtkunstwerk*, the total work of art, which began with the building and included every detail of decoration and furnishing. Wagner's student, Joseph Maria Olbrich, designed the Secession Building in Vienna, while another student from his architectural office, Josef Hoffmann, and the painter Koloman Moser were given responsibility for the arrangement and display of the first Secession Exhibition, held in 1898 in Olbrich's magnificent and richly adorned exhibition hall. By the time of the eighth Secession Exhibition, held in 1900, not only paintings but also decorative arts, including work by Ashbee, de Morgan and Charles Rennie Mackintosh, were included. Secessionist ideas were spread more rapidly among the next generation after the appointment of Hoffmann and Moser as teachers at the Vienna Kunstgewerbeschule (School of Arts and Crafts).

In 1899 architects, artists and designers from all over Europe were called together in the most ambitious Arts-and-Crafts-inspired programme of regeneration yet undertaken, when Ernst Ludwig, a grandson of Queen Victoria who had succeeded to the Grand Duchy of Hesse in 1892 at the age of twenty-three, established an artists' colony on the Mathildenhöhe, a small hill he owned to the north-east of the old town of Darmstadt. Ludwig had travelled in England and seen the work of Arts and Crafts architects and designers. He had invited Otto Eckmann to furnish his private study in the Neue Palais in Darmstadt and the young English architect M. H. Baillie Scott to contribute furniture and decorations for the drawing-room and dining room. Baillie Scott's designs were made by

Ashbee's Guild of Handicraft, and Ashbee had provided the light fittings.

Ludwig believed that he could stimulate the economy of his little country by bringing about a revival of arts and crafts, and so he set about enticing internationally renowned artists to come to Darmstadt. The artists' colony was formally established on 1 July 1899. Olbrich came from Vienna, and Behrens from Munich, together with six other German painters, sculptors and designers, all aged under thirty-three. Ludwig's plans had the useful support of the publisher Alexander Koch, who gave the colony welcome coverage in his magazines, *Zeitschrift für Innen-Dekoration* and *Deutsche Kunst und Dekoration*.

The artists' first scheme was to devise an interior to be shown at the Exposition Universelle in Paris in 1900 for which Olbrich, who emerged as the unelected leader, contributed the overall design. The colony, which ended in 1914, showed its work at various international exhibitions, including Turin in 1902 and St Louis in 1904, but the most important statement of its aims was *Ein Dokument Deutscher Kunst*, staged in 1901, when, in addition to an exhibition held in a special hall designed by Olbrich, the houses and studios designed and furnished by the various colonists were thrown open to the public. The model homes on the Mathildenhöhe made actual the dream of turning daily life into an aesthetic experience. Olbrich's was like a south German farmhouse, with an open entrance porch, carved wooden flower galleries, a tiled roof and a decorative frieze of blue and white tiles across the side of the building. Inside, carved and plain wood was enhanced by

J.M. Olbrich's house,
built in 1901 on the
Mathildenhöhe, Darmstadt

In America, too, Ruskin and Morris were influential figures, though their medieval dreams meant little in a country in the throes of post-Civil War reconstruction, a vast land which had its own potent images in the extension of railroads, the exploration of new territories and the taming the wild frontier. The unpeopled landscapes of the Hudson River painters, the romance of the American Indians, the simplicity of religious sects such as the Shakers were far more compelling to an American public than the Arthurian poetry of Tennyson or Pre-Raphaelite images of 'medieval damozels'. Writers and poets such as Washington Irving, Henry Longfellow or Mark Twain supplied the vocabulary of a primitive, outdoor, pioneer life of simple values and closeness to nature. From the 1880s log-cabins and bungalows began to be popular as weekend or summer retreats for city-dwelling woodsmen and their families, and became to the American Arts and Crafts movement what the country cottage with hollyhocks growing at the gate was in England – a symbol of harmony and spiritual well-being.

In the Yellowstone National Park the Old Faithful Inn was built in 1902 as a log-cabin a mere six storeys high! And hundreds of more modest summer resorts, country clubs and sanatoriums from Florida to Maine, from California to the Adirondacks, were furnished with 'woodsy' tables, settees, chairs and rockers made by firms such as the Old Hickory Furniture Co. in Indiana which used the wood, cane and bark of the region's plentiful hickory trees for porch and garden furniture.

Log-cabins and bungalows, complete

patterned curtains and decorative friezes.

Peter Behrens built a house where every facet of its design, right down to the cutlery, was integrated in terms of an overall coherence of design. It was hailed as introducing a new age of beauty and was a realization of the *Gesamtkunstwerk*, the 'total design work', which united the material skill of the craftsman with the spiritual content of the artist.

with porches and simple, life-affirming mottoes over the fireplace, were among the designs for 'Craftsman Homes' which Gustav Stickley sold by mail in addition to the plans he published in *The Craftsman* magazine; in 1904 he founded the Craftsman Home-Builders Club which offered complete sets of plans to subscribers. The designs, many of which were by the architect Harvey Ellis, were inexpensive and well suited to the suburbs, where they were seen as being in keeping with the landscape as well as being redolent of a masculine, backwoodsy life lived close to nature. In 1909 Henry L. Wilson founded the *Bungalow Magazine* in Los Angeles; this regularly featured complete plans and drawings for a 'bungalow of the month'.

It was Gustav Stickley more than anyone who married the aims of the British Arts and Crafts movement to the frontier style of the log-cabin and produced what was known in America as 'reform' or 'Mission' furniture. In October 1900 the Tobey Furniture Co. of Chicago launched a range of 'New Furniture' designed by Stickley in plain, solid oak and similar to a range of so-called 'Mission' furniture the firm had introduced earlier that year. The term 'Mission', first coined at that time, was never used by Stickley himself, and it is not known whether it was derived from the Franciscan missions of California or from the notion of 'furniture with a mission'. Whatever name it went by, the new style, tagged as 'an unconventional style for unconventional people', proved to be very popular with the public and in 1901, in addition to a new Art Nouveau line, Tobey's catalogue offered 'New Furniture in Weathered Oak'; in 1902, after Stickley set

up his own Craftsman workshops, they introduced the name 'Russmore' for their Mission-style furniture.

The plain, broad oak planks of Stickley's Craftsman furniture, with its leather upholstery and beaten-copper hinges, went well with leaded glass and stencilled decoration – and with the Navajo rugs, patchwork quilts from Appalachian mountain folk, and distinctive blue and white bedspreads from Deerfield, Massachusetts which were sold with Stickley furniture. Stickley's style was widely copied, not least by L. and J. G. Stickley of Fayetteville, New York, the firm founded in 1902 by his younger brothers, Leopold and John George, and Stickley's own Craftsman enterprises reached from coast to coast.

However, despite the handmade, pioneer spirit of his furniture, and the articles he published in *The Craftsman* advocating the values he saw enshrined in the life of the craft workshop, most of the thousands of pieces of furniture produced in the Craftsman workshops were machine-made. Stickley saw his furniture as expressive of a rugged simplicity quite different from the joy in execution treasured by Ashbee or the furniture maker Sidney Barnsley, and he valued its lack of refinement, which he saw as redolent of the American spirit: 'we have no monarchs and no aristocracy,' he wrote, 'the life of the plain people is the life of the nation'. As he explained in 1904: 'the very crudity of my structural plan . . . was to me proof of its vital power . . . decadence is the natural sequence of over-refinement.' And in 1909 he wrote of his Craftsman furniture: 'Like the Arts and Crafts furniture in England, it represented a revolt from the

Living room of the 'nobly barbaric' log house at Gustav Stickley's Craftsman Farms in Morris Plains, New Jersey, illustrated in *The Craftsman*, November 1911. Stickley's plans for a Utopian community in Morris Plains never materialized

machine-made thing. But there is this difference: the Arts and Crafts furniture was primarily intended to be an expression of individuality, and the Craftsman furniture was founded on a return to sturdy and primitive forms that were meant for usefulness alone.'

In 1908 Stickley bought land near Morris Plains in New Jersey, hoping to found a co-operative community to be called the Craftsman Farms, but the plan came to nothing. Other experiments in Arts and Crafts living met with varied success. The Philadelphia architect William L. Price was, with Wilson Eyre (an architect and founder-editor of *House and Garden*), a member of the T-Square Club, which provided a forum for the discussion of Arts and Crafts topics. Their deliberations led Price to found the Rose Valley Community near Philadelphia in 1901 with financial assistance from several prominent Philadelphians, including Edward Bok, founder of the *Ladies' Home Journal*. Price hired immigrant wood-

carvers to make oak furniture to his designs with carved Gothic decoration, using only hand tools. The community also produced bookbindings and pottery. But after five years the woodwork shop closed amid complaints of poor working conditions and Rose Valley degenerated into little more than a cultural centre.

Ralph Radcliffe Whitehead was a wealthy amateur craftsman who had known Ruskin at Oxford and travelled with him in Italy. In 1902 he founded Byrdcliffe on a wooded mountainside near Woodstock, New York, and used his inherited fortune to keep the colony going until his death in 1926. Although Byrdcliffe produced some simple oak furniture, made by professionally trained artists and craftsmen, as well as picture frames, pottery and weaving, it never really prospered, and soon become more or less Whitehead's private estate, 'the shell of a great life', as Ashbee described it on a visit in 1915. Byrdcliffe was to have been devoted to preserving pre-industrial skills, but the mountain streams proved not to be forceful enough to power machinery. Whitehead also believed that living close to nature would enhance the lives of his workers, but, like his mentor Ruskin, he had attempted, in Ashbee's opinion, 'to solve the problem of the Arts and Crafts in the manner of the Grand Seigneur'.

The most successful of the American craft communities was Roycroft, founded in East Aurora, New York, by Elbert Hubbard, a flamboyant and successful salesman who in his mid-thirties retired from his brother-in-law's Buffalo soap business to establish the Roycroft Press in 1895. Hubbard claimed to have been inspired by a visit to

William Morris's Kelmscott Press the previous year, but that may only have been astute salesmanship. Certainly he shared none of Morris' socialist sympathies and was, from the start, outrageously commercial, an 'Anarkist with a K', as Janet Ashbee described him. Roycroft began with a small press, then a bindery and a leatherwork shop were added, and slowly a guild-like community began to take shape. In 1909 a metalwork shop, run by a former banker, Karl Kipp, was opened. The Roycroft Press also published *The Philistine*, a journal which achieved a circulation of over one hundred thousand copies a month.

In 1896 the Roycroft Shops had begun to make furniture for the Roycroft Inn, a place where visitors curious to see the community could stay, and the woodwork shop expanded to produce souvenirs for them to take home. 'They made it as good as they could – folks came along and bought it', was how Hubbard accounted for its existence. By 1901 furniture was offered in the firm's mail-order catalogue. Simple, square, oak pieces, with little ornament, but slightly more Gothic in style than Craftsman furniture, were constructed with pegs, pins and mortise-and-tenon joints and marked with either the orb and cross, the symbol Hubbard had adopted for the Roycroft Press, or an incised 'Roycroft'. In 1908 the Roycroft designer Dard Hunter, already an avid reader of German publications, visited Vienna and subsequently incorporated Wiener Werkstätte motifs into Roycroft products.

Hubbard said that each piece was made to order by individual craftsmen, a highly unlikely claim given the size of the workshops

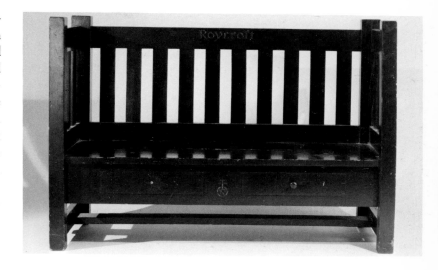

– by 1906 over four hundred people worked there – and the machinery he invested in. Nevertheless, he obviously saw that exclusivity was a good marketing ploy, and constantly alerted his customers to the investment potential of his goods. In 1915, following the death of Elbert Hubbard and his wife aboard the *Lusitania*, their son Bert took over the firm, successfully establishing Roycroft 'departments' in several hundred stores; the Roycroft Shops were finally sold in 1938.

For several years before his death, Hubbard's successful commercialization of the original high ideals of the Arts and Crafts movement had been mirrored in thousands of inferior products made throughout Europe and America, although few firms went to the lengths of establishing both a community and a company magazine to reinforce the apparent 'message' they sold with their wares. For most, a passing visual reference to the style was sufficient to market their products.

Painted oak settee with two drawers, carved with 'Roycroft' and the company's orb mark, c.1910

THE ART CHAIR

As the rage for 'Art' furniture spread, manufacturers produced rival versions of the cheap and popular Art chair. The archetypal Art chair was the rush-seated, turned and spindled, stained 'Sussex' chair produced by Morris and Co. from 1865, and still part of their standard stock when the firm was liquidated in 1940. Ford Madox Brown, who discovered its rural prototype, is traditionally credited with its design, but there is also a variation named the 'Rossetti' chair. A light chair, useful in the dining-room or bedroom, it was also relatively inexpensive – at the turn of the century, for example, it cost only seven shillings (35p) – and could be bought with or without arms, with square or round seat, and with matching settee.

E. W. Godwin's very Japanese-looking ebonized chair design was, he claimed, also based on 'an old English example' and was described in the manufacturer William Watt's catalogue as 'Jacobean', yet it made itself at home in the Aesthetic interiors of Tite Street, Chelsea, or Bedford Park, Chiswick.

Liberty's, of course, also jumped on the bandwagon with an ebonized chair similar to their 'Thebes' stool, which had been designed by Leonard F. Wyburd, based on one by the artist Holman Hunt which had been inspired by an Egyptian original. On the whole, however, it continued to be the English vernacular that inspired these sophisticated items of self-consciously simple furniture. In *Hints on Household Taste*, C. L. Eastlake, recommending the traditional Windsor chair, went so far as to add that, 'We have at the present time no more artistic workman in his way than the country cartwright' – a message very much taken to heart by the furniture designer Ernest Gimson, by Sidney Barnsley and, in the early years of this century, by Ambrose Heal.

C. R. ASHBEE

Above: Silverwares designed by C.R. Ashbee: a silver teapot of 1901; a silver-plated muffin dish; a silver-plated clock with chased decoration; and a cigarette box, c.1904; (*below right*) an embossed copper dish made in 1891 by John Pearson, who had previously worked for the Guild of Handicraft; (*below left*) Ashbee photographed by Frank Lloyd Wright, c.1900

Charles Robert Ashbee (1863–1942) was a fairly typical middle-class undergraduate at Cambridge until he began to read Ruskin and to visit the socialist writer Edward Carpenter at his small farm near Sheffield in the early 1880s. In 1886, the year Ashbee went on from Cambridge to train as an architect in the offices of G. F. Bodley, he went to hear Carpenter lecture to the Hammersmith branch of the Socialist League, and there met William Morris. At this time Ashbee was living at Toynbee Hall in Whitechapel, opened two years earlier to bring undergraduates into contact with people of the East End, and was lecturing there, and at Working Men's Clubs, on Ruskin.

Ashbee's lectures led to his class undertaking the decoration of the dining-room in the new Toynbee Hall buildings, and by the end of 1887 he was planning a craft school and guild. Despite the fact that, when consulted, Morris poured 'a great deal of cold water' on his ideas, the School and Guild of Handicraft were established at Toynbee Hall in June 1888. Ashbee was only twenty-five, and early members included former office clerks and barrow-boys, with only one metalworker, John Pearson, and a cabinet-maker (and active trade unionist) C. V. Adams.

In 1891 the Guild moved to Essex House, an elegant Queen Anne building in the Mile End Road. Ashbee lived there until his marriage, although the regular suppers, outings and entertainments with Guild members continued.

Over the next ten years the Guild grew and acquired new skills, and in 1899 a shop was opened just off Bond Street. Jewellery, inspired by Ashbee's admiration for Italian Renaissance originals, and silver tablewares were always the most popular items. Ashbee used several favourite design motifs; the peacock, the ship, the sun, the tree of life, and the pink, which grew in the garden at Essex House and was adopted as a Guild emblem.

Ashbee worked closely with his silversmiths: craftsman and designer learned new techniques together, finishing silver pieces by planishing with a small round hammer to give a beautiful texture to the surface. The Guild's furniture, too, was remarkable for the quality of the metalwork, and Ashbee's collaboration with Baillie Scott on the furnishings for the Grand Duke of Hesse's palace in Darmstadt did much to refine his style.

In 1896 Ashbee made the first of several visits to America; over the years he met many American designers and architects, including Elbert Hubbard, Charles Sumner Greene and Frank Lloyd Wright, who became a good friend.

Despite the commercial success of the Guild, Ashbee wanted something more from his dream, and in 1902 a democratic decision was taken to remove the Guild and the members' families to Chipping Campden in Gloucestershire where these Londoners could come 'home' to the land. They took over a disused silk mill in the village as workshops, and renovated local houses to live in; they built a swimming-pool in the river, grew their own vegetables and sang folk-songs. But in 1907 the Guild, which at one time numbered 150 working men, women and boys, went into voluntary liquidation, defeated not only by the costs of removal to the country and the difficulty of sending goods to London for sale (for there was no railway nearby), but also by the impossibility of laying men off when orders were thin, as they had been able to do in the city.

Ashbee returned to London, to his architectural practice, more convinced than ever of the need for radical social change in order to allow guilds of the future to survive.

ENTERTAINMENT

Maypole dancing on the village green, an English custom fondly
'remembered' by Arts and Crafts supporters

Nowhere was the Arts and Crafts nostalgia for a lost rural idyll, for 'olde English' hospitality and for a quondam English identity more evident than in the ways in which people enjoyed themselves. Country dances, maypole dancing, morris dancing, ballads, madrigals, Christmas mummers' plays, medieval revels and pageants were all revived, not only in reality but as a source of illustration and decorative motif.

In 1881 Ruskin devised a May Queen ceremony for Whitelands teacher-training college in Chelsea, commissioning gold 'Queen of the May' brooches of hawthorn entwined about a cross from his friends Arthur Severn and Edward Burne-Jones.

In 1885 Walter Crane was involved with a series of tableaux vivants put on by the Royal Society of Painters in Watercolours and entitled 'The Masque of Painters'; twelve years later, another tableau vivant, 'Beauty's Awakening: A Masque of Winter and of Spring', combined his talents with those of C. R. Ashbee, Henry Wilson and other members of the Art Workers' Guild, which had held a meeting on masques and pageants earlier in the year. In Glasgow, too, Fra (Francis) Newbery, principal of the

School of Art, organized masques with his students.

Ernest Gimson and his wife Emily were both interested in traditional English music, and were friendly with both Cecil Sharp, the collector of English folk-songs, and Arnold Dolmetsch, who revived appreciation of early English music, particularly of the recorder. Through the Century Guild in 1892, A. H. Mackmurdo, also a friend of Dolmetsch, organized three concerts of sixteenth- and seventeenth-century music, performed on the viol, lute and harpsichord; Janet Ashbee edited a collection of English folk-songs, the *Essex House Song Book*, published in 1903; Harry Peach, the founder of Dryad Handicrafts, was a prominent member of the Folk Dancing Society.

Ashbee was also a member of the Elizabethan Stage Society, which produced Elizabethan and Jacobean plays according to their original conventions. The contemporary London stage underwent its own revolution, with dramatists such as Oscar Wilde and Arthur Pinero, designers such as Edward Gordon Craig (son of the actress Ellen Terry and E. W. Godwin), and actresses such as Sarah Bernhardt and Eleonora Duse, and Gordon Craig's one-time lover, the dancer Isadora Duncan.

Interior of the Tabard Inn,
Bedford Park, Chiswick, as
it is today

*The Apotheosis of Italian
Art*, by Walter Crane,
1885, from the tableau
vivant 'The Masque of
Painters'. City Art Gallery,
Manchester

PRIVATE PRESSES

Since his undergraduate days, William Morris had been interested in medieval illumination and book production,
and he collected illuminated manuscripts and early printed
books throughout his life. In January 1891 he installed a
second-hand Albion hand-press in his house at Hammersmith, intending to return to first principles, with authentic papers, inks, and typefaces. He was helped in his
researches by his friend Emery Walker, who had advised
the Century Guild on the printing of their magazine *The
Hobby Horse* in 1884, and who went on to found the Doves
Press with T. J. Cobden-Sanderson in 1900. Walker had
lectured at the Arts and Crafts Exhibition Society in 1888
on the importance of book design: 'Type and paper may be
said to be to a printed book, what stone or bricks and mor-
tar are to architecture,' he declared. 'They are the essen-
tials, without which there can be no book.'

Morris's first volume from the Kelmscott Press, *The Glit-
tering Plain*, was published in May 1891; the initial edition
of two hundred copies sold out, and on the basis of his success he moved to bigger premises and installed a second
press. He published over fifty titles before his death in
1896, including his own works, those of Ruskin and
Chaucer, and his own translations of Icelandic sagas and
The Tale of Beowulf. He designed typefaces, such as Golden,
Troy and Chaucer, decorative borders and initials; Burne-
Jones contributed most of the woodblock illustrations.

The success of the Kelmscott Press inspired many other
private presses, such as Charles Ricketts's Vale Press,
Lucien Pissarro's Eragny Press and C. R. Ashbee's Essex
House Press. Like Morris, Ashbee wrote many didactic
pamphlets as well as books, and saw the opportunity of ac-
quiring Morris's old presses, which he bought in 1898, as a
means of publishing his own views in an Arts and Crafts
manner. In 1907 Ananda Coomaraswamy, Ashbee's
neighbour in Chipping Campden, took over the Essex
House Press to publish his own book, *Medieval Sinhalese
Art*. By 1910, when Coomaraswamy left for India, the
Essex House Press had printed more than ninety titles.

In America, more than fifty private presses were estab-

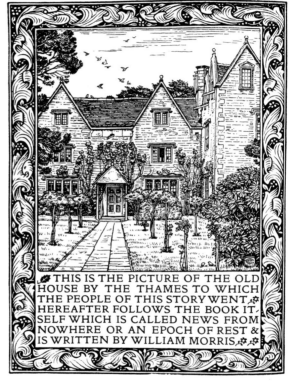

The frontispiece of *News From Nowhere* by William Morris,
Kelmscott Press, 1892, with an illustration of Kelmscott Manor
by Charles March Gere

lished between 1895 and 1910. Daniel Berkeley Updike's
Merrymount Press, founded in Boston in 1893, was one of
the first. Like the Doves Press, Updike introduced a plainer,
more sober style. Other American presses included Elbert
Hubbard's Roycroft Press, Will Bradley's Wayside Press,
the Blue Sky Press in Chicago, the Alwil Press in New Jersey
and Frederic W. Goudy's Village Press, founded in Chicago
in 1903 and moved to Massachusetts the following year.

In Europe, the Kelmscott Press inspired new interest in
typography and printing, for books, magazines and posters,
mainly in the new *Jugendstil* or Art Nouveau style.

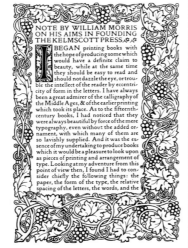

Above: Opening pages of Morris's *Notes* on founding the Kelmscott Press, with illustration by Burne-Jones and 'Golden' type, initial and borders by Morris

Below: Title page from *The Book of Common Prayer*, the Merrymount Press, 1928

Right: Pages from the *Song Book of the Guild of Handicraft*, Essex House Press

THE BOOK OF COMMON PRAYER

and Administration of the Sacraments
and Other Rites and Ceremonies
of the Church

ACCORDING TO THE USE OF THE
PROTESTANT EPISCOPAL CHURCH
IN THE UNITED STATES OF AMERICA

Together with The Psalter
or Psalms of David

PRINTED FOR THE COMMISSION
A. D. MDCCCCXXVIII

MISCELLANY OF SOℲG, IN WHICH ARE INCLUDED SONGS OF THE UNIVERSITIES AND SONGS OF PURE NONSENSE, BEING THE TENTH PART OF THE SONG BOOK OF THE GUILD OF HANDICRAFT.

THE LEATHER BOTTÈL.

16th or 17th Century.

When I survey the world around
The wondrous things that do abound,
The ships that on the sea do swim
To keep our foes that none come in,
Ay! let them all say what they can,
'Twas for one end the use of man,
So I wish him joy where'er he dwell,
That first found out the leather bottèl.

Now what do you say to those cans of wood?
Oh, no, in faith they cannot be good!
For if the bearer fall by the way
Why on the ground your liquor doth lay:
But had it been in a leather bottèl,
Although he had fallen, all had been well:
So I wish him joy where'er he dwell,
That first found out the leather bottèl.

Then what do you say to these glasses fine?
Oh, they shall have no praise of mine!
For if you chance to touch the brim,
Down falls the liquor and all therein,
But had it been in a leather bottèl,
And the stopper in, all had been well:
So I wish him joy where'er he dwell,
That first found out the leather bottèl.
VII.—2

GUSTAV STICKLEY

Above left: Oak reclining chair made in Gustav Stickley's Craftsman Workshops *c.*1905, and based on Morris and Co.'s earlier, successful version; oak bookcase (*below left*), with wrought iron lock plate and handle, designed by Gustav Stickley; and (*far right*) a chest of drawers in oak designed by Harvey Ellis and produced by the Craftsman workshops, *c.*1907

Gustav Stickley (1857–1942) learned his craft from an uncle in Pennsylvania who made wooden and cane-seated chairs, and, during the 1880s, in partnership with his brother, he made and sold reproduction furniture in various styles. However, he came under the influence of a teacher from Syracuse University who admired the writings of Ruskin and Morris, and in 1898 he visited England and saw work by Mackmurdo, Baillie Scott, Voysey and other Arts and Crafts movement designers whose work he knew from the pages of *The Studio* magazine.

On his return to Syracuse, Stickley founded his own company, and in 1901 established United Crafts, intended to be a profit-sharing guild, 'the beginning of a new and unique labor association, a guild of cabinet makers, metal and leather workers, formed for the production of house-hold furnishings', as he described it. In October he launched *The Craftsman* magazine. In its first issue, devoted to William Morris, he wrote that he wanted 'to promote and to extend the principles established by Morris, in both the artistic and the socialistic sense'. Although, as the firm grew, the workers no longer received stock options, and the United Crafts Guild was reorganized and renamed the Craftsman Workshops, Stickley continued for several years to print overtly socialist articles in the *The Craftsman*.

The Craftsman Workshops produced strong, simple, comfortable, plain oak furniture 'in the endeavor', so Stickley wrote in 1901, 'to substitute the luxury of taste for the luxury of costliness'. Some of his early designs owed much to Baillie Scott, and the adjustable reclining chair, produced around 1902, was surely based on a Morris and Co. original. In May 1902 a metalwork shop was opened, making copper handles and strap-hinges for furniture as well as hand-wrought copper vases, jardinières and plaques.

In 1903 Stickley was joined by the architect Harvey Ellis, who refined and lightened the Craftsman style, adding a more subtle and sophisticated sense of mass and line, perhaps partly derived from the work of the Glasgow School designers whose furniture he saw illustrated in *The Studio*. He used less applied metalwork, but introduced conventionalized floral motifs inlaid in pewter, copper and stained and exotic woods. Harvey Ellis died prematurely in January 1904, but his brief influence immensely benefited the furniture made over the next half-dozen years. After 1910 few new designs were introduced.

The Craftsman style struck a chord with the American public and was immensely popular: the mail-order catalogues went all over the United States, and Craftsman furniture could be seen in showrooms from Boston to Los Angeles. But, after a move to New York in 1913, Stickley overextended his growing financial empire and in 1915 went bankrupt: the Craftsman Workshops were amalgamated with his brothers' firm, L. and J. G. Stickley. The last issue of *The Craftsman* was published in December 1916.

An Eclectic Style

A vital influence that tempered the appeal of Gothic just as the Arts and Crafts movement gathered pace was the Aesthetic movement, which brought a lighter, more whimsical, touch to the new style. The Aesthetic movement combined the growing cult for all things Japanese with the developing interest in a revival of the so-called 'Queen Anne' style of architecture, and added its own element of wit, of cultivated artificiality and of decadence. Such an element of modern sophistication was vital: as Richard Norman Shaw, G. E. Street's pupil and the greatest proponent of the 'Queen Anne' revival style, said of Gothic in 1902: 'I am personally devoted to it, admire it in the abstract, and think it superb; but it is totally unsuited to modern requirements. . . .' The influence of the Aesthetic movement prevented the Arts and Crafts from losing themselves in medieval nostalgia.

Japanese arts and crafts were first widely seen in England in 1862 when Sir Rutherford Alcock, Britain's first official representative in Japan, exhibited his personal collection of Japanese lacquer, bronze and porcelain at the International Exhibition in London, for Japan had been closed to the West for many years. Japanese attitudes to design were very much in harmony with the prevailing Western ideas of the time, especially in that oriental art tended to blur the distinctions between the fine and applied arts. Those British artists struggling to escape from the strict demarcations set by the Royal Academy found in Japanese arts not only a welcome simplicity and new forms of representation but also an ancient respect for other media.

One of the first serious collectors of Japanese prints was William Burges, who found in Japanese arts the same freedom of expression and lack of regularity that he most admired in Gothic. His friends D. G. Rossetti and E. W. Godwin were also early collectors. The ebonized couch that Rossetti exhibited in 1862 in the Medieval Court was Japanese-inspired, and Godwin, then living in Bristol, was one of the very first to decorate his home in the Japanese taste, with *tatami* mats on the floor, Japanese fans and prints (bought in the early 1860s) on the walls, and blue and white vases. Nevertheless, Godwin, like Burges and Rossetti, managed to combine all manner of influences, from Gothic to Greek. In 1867, for example, he incorporated Japanese peacock and sun motifs in a Gothic castle built in Ireland for the Earl of Limerick.

Woven silk 'Butterfly' brocade, designed by E. W. Godwin, c.1874. Victoria & Albert Museum, London

Wallpaper, frieze, filling and dado designed by Bruce Talbert for Jeffrey and Co. in 1887. Victoria & Albert Museum, London

In the 1870s Godwin designed furniture and interiors for his friends, Oscar Wilde and James McNeill Whistler, both of whom lived in Tite Street, Chelsea, and also for the actresses Ellen Terry (by whom he had two children) and Lillie Langtry. The White House at 35 Tite Street was designed for Whistler in 1877; in its lightness and simplicity, it was a far cry from the designs for town halls and Gothic castles he had worked on in the previous decade. The red brick and white woodwork of other similar houses in Tite Street were typical of the new 'Queen Anne' style, not only in their tall, irregular windows, either leaded or enhanced with white glazing bars, but also in their gables, dormers and ornate chimneys. Norman Shaw, the most famous practitioner of this comfortable, light and supposedly hygienic middle-class style, set up his own architectural office in London in 1862, and his clients, too, included such luminaries of the Aesthetic movement as Kate Greenaway, for whom he built a house in Hampstead in 1885; in 1877 he had succeeded Godwin as estate architect at Bedford Park, London's first 'garden suburb'.

Perfection was an essential ingredient of the Aesthetic style, and Godwin oversaw the decoration of Oscar Wilde's house himself. One room was painted in different shades of white and the palest grey, and the dramatist described the dining-room chairs as 'sonnets in ivory', the table as a 'masterpiece in pearl'. In 1874, when decorating the house he shared in Harpenden with Ellen Terry, Godwin had even mixed his own paints – a dark-toned yellow and a pale grey-green, which he described as 'that green sometimes seen at the stem end of a

Stoneware pot with incised decoration of lilies and a dragonfly, made by the Martin Brothers in 1884

pineapple leaf when the other end has faded – indeed I may as well confess that most of the colours in the rooms have been gathered from the pineapple'. Another room, 'almost entirely furnished with Japanese things', was done in shades of blue, and, in the hall, the floorboards were waxed and left bare, the walls were of creamy vellum and the paintwork light red – a stunningly modern combination.

While it was probably Whistler who inspired Godwin's colour sense, it was Oscar Wilde who did most to ally the Aesthetic movement to new developments in literature and poetry. In France, Baudelaire had translated the works of Edgar Allan Poe, while Proust translated Ruskin; Wilde in turn took works by Huysmans and de Montesquieu and popularized them, in 1891, in *The Picture of Dorian Gray*. The notion common to all these writers, and also, earlier, to Walter Pater and, subsequently, to Henry James, was that beautiful objects had the power to evoke moods and feelings in the beholder. The French theory of *correspondances* held that objects of specially heightened significance – Wilde claimed that, for him, it was blue and white china, but for other aesthetes it might have been a Japanese fan, a sunflower or a lily – were beautiful only in that they reflected and enhanced the passion of the spectator. According to Wilde, 'It is the spectator, and not life, that art really mirrors.'

In self-conscious England, such aesthetic philosophies were doomed to be short-lived. People who worshipped blue and white porcelain, or peacock feathers and used Japanese parasols as summer firescreens were lampooned by W. S. Gilbert in

Patience, first produced in 1881, and, as the Cimabue Browns, in George du Maurier's *Punch* cartoons. In England, too, the much vaunted admiration of the Aesthetes for decadence and unnaturalness was seen to degenerate into a series of rows and scandals: an attack by Ruskin on Whistler's paintings led to a celebrated libel case, Rossetti retreated into drug abuse, and Oscar Wilde was imprisoned for homosexuality. In France, on the other hand, Baudelaire's poems inspired a series of magnificent vases by the glass designer Emile Gallé, who also greatly admired Japanese art, and Art Nouveau designers such as Louis Majorelle and Hector Guimard thrived upon the intensity of such decadent ideas.

The English Aesthetic movement, perhaps typified by the work of Lewis F. Day, Walter Crane and Thomas Jekyll, remained essentially light, pretty and elegant. Jekyll, who went insane in 1877 and died four years later, executed woodwork for the Liverpool

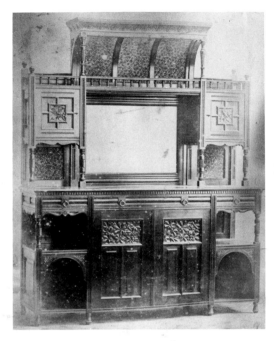

directorship of W. S. Coleman, whose own simpering ceramic portraits of Aesthetic nymphs highlight the gulf between English prettiness and the brooding intensity of French Art Nouveau. However, the Martin Brothers, at their pottery in Southall, turned out stoneware decorated with naturalistic Japanese-inspired plants, birds, fish and insects which showed a true understanding of the basis of Japanese motifs. Edwin Martin also produced abstract vases in the strong, muted colours of stoneware that, by their shape and texture, suggested natural vegetable or marine forms. And at Farmer and Rogers Emporium, which sold all manner of exotic imported items, the oriental manager, Arthur Lasenby Liberty, realized that there was a healthy market for furnishings in the new style; after twelve years' service, he left in 1875 to set up his own store, Liberty and Co.

In the winter of 1881 Oscar Wilde, the 'ultra poetical, super-aesthetical, soul-eyed young man', arrived, lilies in hand, on the shores of America. His lecture tour was greeted with delight, for the Americans had already begun their own Aesthetic movement after both Japanese and modern European arts and crafts had been widely seen at the 1876 Centennial Exposition in Philadelphia. Japanese pottery, porcelain and prints, displayed in the Japanese pavilion, were shown at the Philadelphia Exposition, as were such Anglo-Japanese-style pieces as Godwin's furniture designs for Collinson and Lock. American manufacturers such as Mitchell and Rammelsberg of Cincinnati or Kimbel and Cabus of New York had themselves begun to adopt some of the visual idioms of the Anglo-Japanese style, and

shipping magnate Frederick Leyland; this formed part of the original scheme for the room in Leyland's house at 49 Princes Gate, hung with priceless embossed Spanish leather – a wallcovering that Whistler then obliterated, unasked, with turquoise and gold peacocks. Jekyll was best known for his cast-iron fire grates, often set with blue and white tiles, and enhanced with Japanese-inspired swirls or butterflies.

Japanese design led to the simplification of line and colour in textile design as well as to the adoption of oriental motifs; Godwin, Bruce Talbert and Christopher Dresser all created Aesthetic-style fabrics. In ceramics, too, the influence of Japan was strong, and Wedgwood, Worcester, and Minton all produced porcelains in the Aesthetic taste. In 1871 Minton's Art-Pottery Studio was established in Kensington Gore under the

Japanese-inspired white-and-gilt Worcester vase, 1884, photographed on a
silk textile by Bruce Talbert, designed for the 1876 Philadelphia Exhibition

ebonized furniture enhanced with gilt was exhibited alongside the plain oak of the American 'Eastlake' or 'Modern Gothic' manner. Kimbel and Cabus, for example, displayed an entire drawing room furnished in ebonized cherry at the exhibition.

The best American Aesthetic movement furniture was made by Herter Brothers of New York. In 1860 Christian Herter, who was born in Stuttgart, joined the cabinet-making firm that his older brother, Gustave, had founded three years earlier in New York. In the mid-1860s Christian returned to Paris, where he had earlier studied, and also visited England in the early 1870s. Gustave retired in 1870, and over the next few years the younger Herter, aided by William B. Bigelow, the architect in charge of the design department, produced furniture to a high standard of craftsmanship in a variety of revival styles, including Modern Gothic. By the time that Christian retired to Paris in 1880, Herter Brothers were producing their finest Anglo-Japanese pieces with incised and gilded carving and inlaid woods and metals, as well as supplying furnishing fabrics, mosaic, light fittings and imported wallpapers and decorative objects.

Herter Brothers' clients in these years included the American financial magnates William H. Vanderbilt, J. Pierpont Morgan and Jay Gould, as well as Broadway stars such as Lillian Russell who played in Gilbert and Sullivan's comic operas. Their furniture, in cherry or rosewood, inlaid with asymmetrical marquetry designs in lighter woods, used Japanese-style flowers and other motifs to elegant and beautiful effect. Christian Herter died in 1883, but the firm continued in business until the turn of the century, working in a variety of styles.

The range of influences introduced by the Centennial Exposition varied from the Gothic Revival and Arts and Crafts to Japanese design or French Art Nouveau, and by the 1890s Americans could choose happily between a wide diversity of home-produced furnishings. Ties with France during the earlier part of the century had been strong in many branches of the arts, most especially in architecture, but the Centennial celebrations encouraged a revival of interest in the American 'old colonial' furnishings of the previous century. In combination with the 'Shingle' style of the architectural firm McKim, Mead and White and the work of the Boston architect H. H. Richardson, which broke with the prevailing taste for ornate Renaissance revival buildings, the Americans now introduced a simplicity and lightness into domestic architecture, similar to the English 'Queen Anne' revival.

In 1876 Dr Christopher Dresser visited America *en route* for Japan, where he was to advise the Japanese Ministry of the Interior on the display of European artefacts in the Imperial Museum, and on adapting crafts to machine production. He had already been commissioned by a merchant in London to make a collection of Japanese goods, and, in New York, Tiffany and Co. requested a similar collection. Following his visit, some of Dresser's own metalwork designs incorporated added Japanese decoration, but it was Tiffany's chief silversmith and silver designer, Edward C. Moore, who most fully exploited the Japanese use of hand-crafted textural effects and their combinations of precious and coloured base metals, where silver and gold contrasted with brass and

Far right: Coffee set in silver, decorated in other metals, by Tiffany and Co., New York

Right: Vase decorated by Matthew Daly at the Rookwood Pottery, Cincinnati, Ohio in 1899

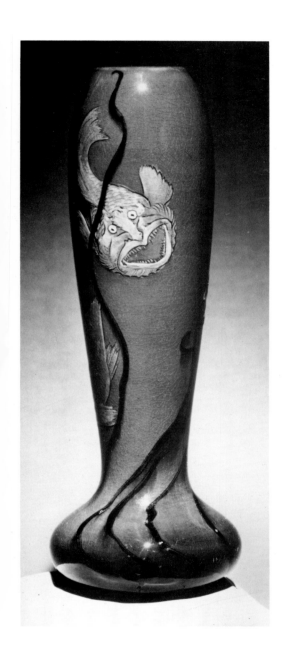

copper. Moore, who before Dresser's visit to Japan had already amassed an extensive reference library and collection, first began using Japanese motifs in the late 1860s; in the 1870s he established a distinctive Aesthetic style, using oriental flowers, vines, gourds, fish and dragonflies made of contrasting metals, and sometimes combining such effects with restrained forms of Art Nouveau.

In 1869 Tiffany's rival, the Gorham Co. of Providence, Rhode Island, also began to produce silver in the Anglo-Japanese style, as did the Whiting Manufacturing Co. of North Attleboro, Massachusetts. In 1897 Gorham launched their 'Martelé' (meaning 'hammered') range under the direction of an Englishman, William Codman. The tea- and coffee-services, fruit dishes and vases in the Martelé range used undulating, natural forms inspired by Art Nouveau.

In ceramics, too, the range of inspiration was diverse. Such visitors to the 1876 Centennial Exposition as Maria Longworth Nichols and M. Louise McLaughlin learned of new methods and techniques from the work of Taxile Doat at Sèvres and Ernest Chaplet at Limoges, from Royal Doulton and Minton's Art-Pottery and from the porcelains in the Japanese pavilion. It was not until 1887, however, seven years after she had founded the Rookwood Pottery, that Nichols employed her first non-American craftsman, the young Kataro Shirayama-dani. In 1893, at Rookwood's request, he returned to Japan to study local glazing techniques, and his decorative motifs – carp, wading birds, and chrysanthemum- and peony-like flowers – remained popular long after Oscar Wilde's trail-blazing tour of the early 1880s had been forgotten.

'Peony' stained glass window by John La Farge, c.1893–1908

The American Aesthetic movement produced one unique art form – the leaded glass designed by John La Farge and Louis Comfort Tiffany. Morris and Co. glass had first been introduced to America by an associate of Bruce Talbert, Daniel Cottier, who opened a shop in New York in 1873 selling Morris and Co. furnishings and ecclesiastical glass. Cottier went on to work with H. H. Richardson, contributing windows to his Trinity Church in Boston, where he was also technical adviser to John La Farge.

La Farge was a lawyer who wanted to become a painter. He visited Europe in the late 1850s, when he also began to collect Japanese prints, and again in the early 1870s, when he met several of the Pre-Raphaelite painters and saw the work of Morris and Co. In 1875 he carried out his first experiments with stained glass, and the following year met Daniel Cottier in Boston. In 1878 he began to design sumptuous windows for private clients, including Cornelius Vanderbilt II in New York and Sir Lawrence Alma-Tadema in London, and by the time of his death in 1906 had produced several thousand windows. Influenced by Japanese prints (he published his impressions of a visit to Japan in *An Artist's Letters from Japan* in 1886), he designed flat, asymmetrical flowers with no painted detail, using instead layered or plated glass, including white opalescent glass, to add subtleties of colour and richness of texture. The shimmering irregularities of the glass alone give a suggestion of depth to the bold blossoms and ornate backgrounds of his designs.

La Farge's technical achievements inspired his more famous successor, L. C. Tiffany, in his experiments with both leaded and blown glass. Tiffany started in business in 1879 as an interior decorator in a partnership named L. C. Tiffany and Associated Artists. The other members of the firm were Candace Wheeler, who was responsible for textiles, George Coleman, an expert in oriental textiles, and Lockwood de Forest, who specialized in carved and ornamental woodwork. Clients included Samuel Clemens ('Mark Twain'), an old friend of Mrs Wheeler's, the English actress, Lillie Langtry, for whose bed they made a silken canopy 'with loops of full-blown, sunset-coloured roses' and a coverlet of 'the delicatest shade of rose-pink satin, sprinkled plentifully with rose petals fallen from the wreaths above', and President Arthur, for whom they revamped the White House.

Candace Wheeler was a woman in her early fifties, a friend of many artists and writers, including John La Farge, F. E. Church and Frederick Law Olmstead, who designed New York's Central Park and pioneered the establishment of the National Parks. Impressed by the work of London's Royal School of Art Needlework exhibited at the 1876 Centennial Exposition, she had founded both the New York Society of Decorative Art to sell needlework, painting, wood-carving and china-painting executed by women, and the Women's Exchange, which sold anything women could produce. She developed the 'needleweaving' technique, patented in 1882, to obtain the naturalistic, painterly effects sought by Tiffany for *portières*, curtains and other hangings.

Tiffany himself was strongly influenced at this time by Moorish architecture, and he contributed the pierced metalwork screens and staircases that added an air of the *Arabian Nights* to Associated Artists' early interiors. Work on the Veterans' Room and Library for the Seventh Regiment Armory on Park Avenue, for example, carried out in 1879–80, combined carved oak panelling, scrolling ironwork, turquoise tiles in the fireplace, a frieze of silver, stencilled silver arabesques, five stained-glass panels and embroidered *portières* to create a rich, textured, sumptuous effect that made real the intense, artistic interiors described by Poe, Wilde or Huysmans.

Despite the success of Associated Artists, in 1883 the four partners went their separate ways; Candace Wheeler continued to run the decorating business until her retirement in 1900. Tiffany became increasingly involved in his experiments with glass. So successful were the productions of Tiffany Studios – windows, lamps, vases – and, like the glass of Gallé or Daum Frères in France, so in keeping with the style of the *fin de siècle*, that they were widely copied: in 1901 two former employees started their own firm, the Quezal Art Glass and Decorating Co. of Brooklyn, and in 1904 the Steuben Glass Works in New York first produced their 'Aurene' range in direct imitation of Tiffany's 'Favrile' glass.

By 1900, in both painting and design, the lessons absorbed from Japanese art had been transmuted into new forms and ideas, but it is worth remembering how revolutionary the use of flat perspectives seemed at the time, not to mention the lack of detail and the asymmetrical arrangements, and how great a challenge the new work of those painters who admired Japanese forms, such as Whistler, Van Gogh or Toulouse-Lautrec, was to the established art world.

Opposite: Silver presentation vase with engraved decoration made by the Gorham Company of Providence, Rhode Island in 1881

E. W. GODWIN

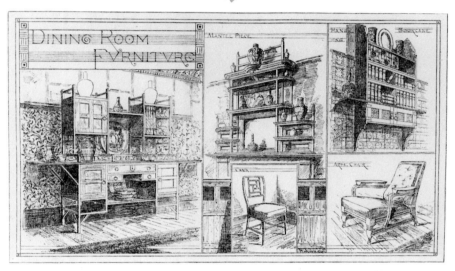

Art furniture for the dining room designed by E.W. Godwin and illustrated in William Watt's
catalogue in 1877

The architect Edwin William Godwin (1833–86) designed his first pieces of furniture when he moved his architectural practice from Bristol to London in the mid-1860s and required inexpensive furniture for his new chambers. By looking at Japanese prints, Godwin had studied the way in which Japanese furniture was constructed, and the fine struts in his designs were inspired by these woodcuts and by *shoji* or *fusama* screens. 'There were to be no mouldings,' he wrote later in 1876, 'no ornamental metal work, no carving. Such effect as I wanted I endeavoured to gain, as in economical building, by the mere grouping of solid and void and by more or less broken outline.'

These early pieces of Anglo-Japanese furniture – a sideboard, side-table and chair, made in ebonized deal – remain his most famous designs, and were later manufactured by William Watt and by Collinson and Lock, and pirated by many other manufacturers. Later, searching for lightness and strength, he used mahogany rather than deal.

In July 1872 he entered into an exclusive three-year contract with Collinson and Lock, Art furnishers, to provide designs not only for furniture but also for fireplaces, gas brackets, lock plates, iron bedsteads and carpets. They parted company before the end of three years, although Collinson and Lock produced rosewood furniture to his designs long afterwards. And in 1877 Watt produced a catalogue of inexpensive Art furniture designed by Godwin.

Sometimes Godwin incorporated in his furniture actual fragments of Japanese ivory, leather-like embossed paper or wooden carved panels (some of them bought at Arthur Lasenby Liberty's new emporium), as well as painted panels by such friends as Whistler, Burne-Jones, Albert Moore and Burne-Jones's pupil Charles Fairfax Murray. At the Paris Exposition Universelle in 1878 he exhibited a group of furniture decorated by Whistler with abstract Japanese-inspired cloud forms.

Godwin's designs for textiles and wallpapers, too, were often based on motifs from Japanese silks, such as a peacock, or the flowering bamboo used for a wallpaper for Jeffrey and Co., and he also designed tiles for Burmantoft and for Minton and Hollins in the new Anglo-Japanese taste.

CHRISTOPHER DRESSER

Dr Christopher Dresser (1834–1904) was every inch the Victorian self-made man, hard-working, talkative and opportunistic. He had entered the Government School of Design when he was thirteen, by the age of twenty-one was lecturing on botany in the provincial Schools, and in the 1860s held professorships in botany both at the South Kensington Museum and at St Mary's School of Medicine. He believed that design should be based upon scientific evidence and principle, and his first books, *Unity in Variety*, 1859, and *The Art of Decorative Design*, 1862, championed the doctrine of conventionalization.

He was a prolific designer, contributing his first freelance designs for textiles, carpets, ceramics and wallpapers to manufacturers such as Brinton and Lewis, Minton, and Wedgwood in the late 1860s. He employed several students and designers in his studio, but all the work went out under his name.

In the 1870s he began designing silver and electroplate for Elkington's, Hukin and Heath and, in 1879, for James Dixon and Son of Sheffield. His sparse, severe designs were quite radical; refusing to compromise with traditional tastes, he had written in 1873: 'In order to its existence [*sic*] a vessel must be constructed but when formed it need not of necessity be ornamented'. His revolutionary metalwork designs are among the earliest celebrations of an industrial aesthetic.

In June 1879, following his trip to America and Japan, Dresser opened a warehouse for Japanese goods in Farringdon Road with Charles Holme (who later founded *The Studio*), and in 1880 he set up the Art Furnishers' Alliance in New Bond Street, with himself as principal designer and 'Art Manager', but despite the craze for all things Aesthetic, both projects were short-lived. However, his time with the Art Furnishers' Alliance did afford Dresser the opportunity to make his début in designing furniture, some of it in the Egyptian style. He also designed cast-iron garden and hall furniture, such as umbrella stands, tables and coat stands, for the Shropshire iron-founders, Coalbrookdale. In 1882 he published a book on his Japanese visit: *Japan: its Architecture, Art and Art Manufactures.*

The energetic Dr Dresser had also been instrumental in setting up the Linthorpe Pottery, established in Yorkshire in 1879, and he remained responsible for design until 1882, when Linthorpe's manager, Henry Tooth, who had also developed most of the glazes, left to go into partnership with William Ault. When Ault founded his own pottery in 1887, Dresser was once again involved.

In the mid-1890s, when he was nearing retirement, Dresser mastered yet another medium when the Glasgow firm of James Couper and Sons began a new venture with the introduction of their 'Clutha' glass. George Walton also designed Clutha glass, but the most distinctive designs were by Dresser and show a rare, romantic sensitivity to natural forms and rhythms. Like L. C. Tiffany, he was influenced by Roman and Middle-Eastern glass, and the blown pieces of opaque green glass, in sinuous, twisted shapes, are often shot with translucent streaks of gold or cream.

'Clutha' glass vase; a silver-plated crow's foot Hukin and Heath claret jug of Egyptian inspiration, 1881; a Wedgwood pottery vase, *c.*1885; a three-legged copper kettle made by Benham and Froud, *c.*1885; and a Linthorpe pot, all designed by Christopher Dresser. Private collection, Birkenhead

Overleaf, left: 'Lava' glass vases, L.C. Tiffany's expressionistic simulation of the effects of volcanic forces on glass. The black surface, enhanced with gold lustre, was created by the addition of basalt or talc to the molten glass. Howarth Art Gallery, Accrington

Overleaf, right: The Veterans' Room and Library of the Seventh Regiment Armoury on Park Avenue, New York, decorated by L.C. Tiffany and Associated Artists in 1879–80

LOUIS COMFORT TIFFANY

Anyone who was anybody in America at the turn of the century had a Tiffany window, lamp or mosaic in their home, or donated one to their local church, bank or college. Edgar Allan Poe could almost have been thinking of a Tiffany lamp which 'throws a tranquil but magical radiance over all', when he wrote his essay 'The Philosophy of Furniture', and Tiffany himself certainly believed in the value of stained glass which could fill otherwise drab interiors with warmth and light.

Louis Comfort Tiffany (1848–1933) was the son and heir of the founder of the famous American jewellery store, with his own exotic studio on the top floor of his father's New York mansion. He had studied painting under George Inness and travelled widely in Europe and North Africa. After the break with Associated Artists in 1883, he set up the Tiffany Glass Company, making stained-glass windows and also mosaic, tiles, glass plaques and lustred pieces for such architectural details as doorways, fireplaces and decorative friezes. In 1900, when Tiffany Studios reached their peak, the company also began to produce metalwork, enamelling and bronzes and, from 1904, pottery.

In 1892 he had bought his own glass furnaces at Corona, near New York, and began his experiments with the chemistry of glass-making. In 1895 the first leaded-glass lamps on bronze bases were sold to the public. However, not all the lamps – with names like Wisteria, Acorn, Dragonfly – were designed by Tiffany himself, and the firm continued to make them well into the 1930s after Tiffany had retired.

In 1896, the first 'Favrile' (meaning 'handmade') glass vases went on sale. Tiffany employed many different glass-making techniques, influenced not only by the carved cameo and intaglio decoration of the work of Emile Gallé, which he had seen at the Paris Exposition Universelle in 1889, but also by the ancient examples from his own extensive collection of Roman and Middle-Eastern glass, such as millefiori and lustre. He also perfected his own unique finishes, such as 'Cypriote', which imitated the pitted, corroded surface of excavated Roman glass, and 'Lava', with thick runs of gold dripping down a black body. His Favrile vases glow with colour, from the delicate green and white tracery of vine leaves on the intaglio glass, to bright turquoise, from vivid orange and iridescent gold, to sombre browns, blues and blacks; his forms, too, reflect his rather dream-like sensibility, both gentle and extravagant.

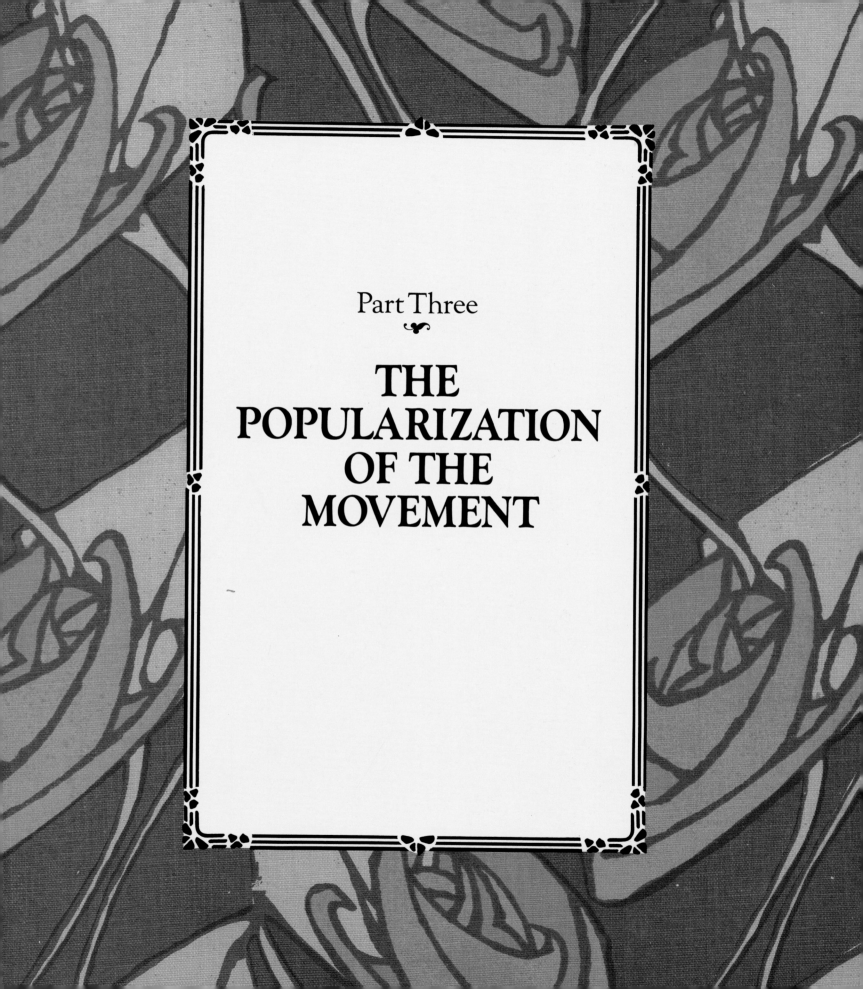

Part Three

THE
POPULARIZATION
OF THE
MOVEMENT

The Refinement of the Style

As the Arts and Crafts movement reached maturity, it attained greater domestic elegance and coherence, concentrating far more on the middle-class home than on the grand interiors of the early Morris and Co. commissions. Gothic, too, was left behind, as the romance of chivalry and medieval hospitality gave way to a more manageable conception of domestic pleasures. The Arts and Crafts house symbolized warmth and shelter, informality and welcome, and was inspired no longer by Gothic cathedrals but by the cottage and the farmhouse.

Rural traditions, vernacular architecture, local materials – these were the elements employed by architects such as Philip Webb, C. F. A. Voysey and Edwin Lutyens in England, by Frank Lloyd Wright, and Greene and Greene in America, or Eliel Saarinen in Finland. Rough-cast stucco, tile-hanging, shingles, half-timbering, patterned brickwork, mullioned and leaded windows were all used to place a building within its particular landscape and to enhance the ornamental role of structural elements. At this time, too, architects began to take greater interest in landscaping their sites, thus provoking a fierce debate in England over the proper role of the architect in garden design.

The first house to break with the imitative historicism of the nineteenth century and create an environment for a modern family had been Philip Webb's Red House, built in 1859 for William Morris. Morris required none of the formality demanded by mid-Victorian social conventions, and passionately desired a home that was beautiful, practical and redolent of his dreams and ideals. The embroideries and furniture that he, Janey and their friends made for the house led to the setting up of Morris, Marshall, Faulkner and Co., and set a precedent that was followed by every Arts and Crafts architect. Morris later had plans to extend the house, to provide workshops for the firm and living quarters for Burne-Jones and his family, although this never happened.

By 1891, when Webb came to design Standen, in Sussex, for the London solicitor, James Beale, his ideas had refined even further. It was said that Webb was never satisfied with a building until it began to look commonplace. The exterior of Standen gives the impression almost of a collection of buildings that have grown together over time, linked by different shapes and textures – brick, stone, tile-hanging, weather-boarding and pebble-dash. Inside, the decorative elements are reticent and

The dining-room at Standen, Sussex, built by Philip Webb and originally furnished by Morris and Co.

M.H. Baillie Scott's prize-winning design for the Music Room for a 'House for an Art Lover', a competition held by the *Zeitschrift für Innendekoration* in 1901. Victoria & Albert Museum, London

understated, with many built-in cupboards, sideboards and benches: Webb even specified the colour of much of the paintwork, such as the distinctive blue-green in the dining-room. He commissioned metalwork from John Pearson, who had been associated with Ashbee's Guild, and light fittings from W. A. S. Benson (Standen was one of the first private houses to be completely electrified from its inception); the decoration of the house was carried out by Morris and Co.

Gradually the Arts and Crafts house came to be increasingly characterized by its internal features such as staircases or fireplaces. Sometimes the work was commissioned from individual or specialist firms – for example, the house that Halsey Ricardo designed at 8 Addison Road, Holland Park, for the department store owner Sir Ernest Debenham incorporated tiles by his former partner, William de Morgan, decorative plasterwork by Ernest Gimson and exterior tiles by Doulton's – but with growing frequency architects themselves were designing more of the details of decoration, from door furniture or stained glass to carpets and curtains.

In 1892 the foundation stone was laid for another Red House, this one built for himself by the architect M. H. Baillie Scott on the outskirts of Douglas, Isle of Man. Baillie Scott had come from Kent to the Isle of Man in 1889, and once there won several commissions for private houses. He had already designed a summer residence for the young Crown Princess Marie of Romania, sister-in-law of the Grand Duke Ernst Ludwig of Hesse, and, through the drawings and watercolour schemes for interiors that he later regularly sent to *The Studio*, his work

became well known and much admired in Europe.

Baillie Scott's compact Red House bears little resemblance to Webb's radical building. On the outside, its traditional half-timbered and tile-hung brickwork is enlived by decorated eaves and by gargoyles squatting on the drainpipes. It is the interior, however, that most clearly shows not only the architect's attention to detail (for example in the fireplace, plasterwork and stained-glass panels), but also his imaginative and informal use of space with, downstairs, panelled walls between the hall, dining-room and drawing-room which slide open to give one large area for entertaining, and, upstairs, a top-lit, panelled gallery from which the bedrooms open out, the whole scheme making a modest house seem airy and roomy.

His later buildings, while still making use of gabled roofs, casement windows or inglenooks, are less self-consciously quaint. Baillie Scott described the home as an 'enchanted realm' and his colourful interiors retain a story-book quality about them. He designed somewhat box-like furniture, decorated with broad, simple patterns and motifs that appear to have their basis in folk traditions, and he often echoed his chosen motifs in stained glass or metalwork. In describing his work, but mistaking his origins, Hermann Muthesius wrote: 'We seem . . . to have stepped into the world of fantasy and romance of the ancient bardic poetry. . . . With Baillie Scott we are among the purely northern poets among British architects.'

It was C. F. A. Voysey who left behind the story-book content of decoration and

Lithograph of Newton Grove, Bedford Park in 1882, by J. Nash, who lived at 36 The Avenue

refined the middle-class house to a basic but easeful simplicity by taking control of every element of an interior. Like Pugin, whose work he greatly admired, he thought that decoration should have meaning. He was particularly interested in the evocative power of symbols, but he integrated the use of such favourite decorative motifs as the stylized heart with strong architectural features. He believed that a house had to provide both physical and spiritual shelter, and the qualities possessed by a home should, he wrote, include 'Repose, Cheerfulness, Simplicity ... Quietness in a storm ... Evidence of Protection ... and making the house a frame to its inmates.'

Voysey specialized in building individual houses set in their own grounds, and could make full use of local materials and traditions; however, in the years after the First World War, his distinctive low-slung roofs and dormer windows were widely copied in suburban housing, which also imitated Baillie Scott's use of black and white timberwork. Just as Ashbee had spoken of his East End Guild workers going 'home' to the land, so increasing numbers of city-dwellers dreamt of a nobler life lived in a cottage with roses round the door, much as Morris had depicted in 1890 in his Utopian romance, *News From Nowhere*, where the socialist future was exclusively rural. By 1900, indeed, the Arts and Crafts movement had come to symbolize a new Utopianism, based on the 'rediscovery' of a supposedly lost rural past. In fact, the rural areas of Britain had been in decline for decades, and by 1900 more than half the population had left the often bleak conditions of the land to live in cities, but the

notion persisted that an earlier rural golden age had been somehow decayed by industrialization and must now be restored.

The Arts and Crafts movement which had championed the rediscovery of lost arts now turned its attention to other manifestations of traditional rural culture (from cider-making to maypole dancing, from folk music to corn dollies), an interest reflected in the writings of Thomas Hardy or John Masefield and in the music of Vaughan Williams and Elgar. As the First World War approached, the 'Englishness' of this revival of folk culture was increasingly allied to patriotism.

One reflection of this dissatisfaction with city life came in 1898 when Ebenezer Howard published *Tomorrow: A Peaceful Path to Social Reform*, revised in 1902 as *Garden Cities of Tomorrow*. In 1899 Howard founded the Garden City Association, which led to the planning and building of the original garden city, at Letchworth, Hertfordshire, in 1903–4.

The first experiment in the creation of an 'aesthetic Eden', with five hundred houses, a kindergarten, other day schools, an art school, co-operative stores, a church and a club was not a garden city but an artistic suburb – Bedford Park in west London. In the 1870s Jonathan T. Carr, a cloth merchant, bought twenty-four acres of land with the intention of building a middle-class Aesthetic estate. His brother, J. W. Comyns Carr, was an art critic and a director of the influential Grosvenor Gallery, and may well have advised on the choice of E. W. Godwin as estate architect. Godwin began designing houses for Bedford Park in 1875 but resigned after criticism of his designs –

the kitchens were said to be poorly planned and the stairs and passageways narrow – and was replaced in 1877 by Norman Shaw. He, too, resigned two years later, although it is thought that he continued as consultant on the project. His successor was E. J. May.

Artists were encouraged to settle in Bedford Park by the provision of studios. Shaw had built several houses for artists, and, to some extent, the irregular disposition of windows in some of his plans was determined by an artist's need of light; certainly his airy, informal interiors suited their modern outlook on life. The Bedford Park houses were advertised as being light, practical and, above all, healthy. The poet W. B. Yeats, the playwright Arthur Pinero, the actor 'Squire' Bancroft, the wallpaper and textile designer C. J. Haité, and even a genuine Russian anarchist were all early residents; Voysey, too, lived there briefly.

Many different designers and manufacturers were involved on the project. The 'old-fashioned' Tabard Inn, designed by Shaw, had tiles by Walter Crane and William de Morgan. The club, by E. J. May, had furniture by Morris and Godwin, with de Morgan tiles and Japanese wallpaper. It not only provided tennis courts but also arranged theatricals, balls and masquerades. Women could also be members, and debates were held there on women's suffrage. Bedford Park received a great deal of publicity – and satiric comment – and other suburbs were quickly built in emulation, such as the Telford Avenue estate in Streatham, south London.

Appalled by the grim conditions of city slums, some industrialists built estate villages for their workers: for example, Port Sunlight in Lancashire or the Bourneville village near Birmingham, developed by the chocolate manufacturer George Cadbury in the 1890s. In 1902 the architects Barry Parker and Raymond Unwin were involved in the Rowntree model village at New Earswick near York, built by the Liberal chocolate manufacturer B. Seebohm Rowntree.

Parker and Unwin had set up in practice in Buxton in 1896. Unwin was Parker's second cousin and in 1893 had married Parker's sister. Both were committed socialists who had been strongly influenced by the writings and example of Edward Carpenter, the original proponent of the 'Simple Life', who lived on his own smallholding near Sheffield. Unwin and his family, like Carpenter, wore specially made sandals, homespun tweeds and 'Ruskin' flannels from the Isle of Man.

Unwin's desire to establish a socialist Utopia led him to become increasingly concerned with town planning and working-class housing. He found himself in tune with Ebenezer Howard's writings on social reform, and with the MP Jesse Collings's 'Back to the Land' movement, which aimed to re-create an ancient yeomanry by encouraging smallholdings. In 1904 Unwin and Parker developed the plans for Letchworth, the first garden city, and went themselves to live there. Their dream was for all classes to live side by side and enjoy the lifestyle of the English country house. Indeed, some of the houses at Letchworth were designed by Baillie Scott, whom Parker greatly admired.

In 1906 Parker and Unwin were involved in the planning of Hampstead Garden Suburb, a community for all classes in north London; however, Edwin Lutyens was

Forest Hills Gardens, Queens in 1914, looking along the arcade towards the inn designed by Grosvenor Atterbury

dens in Queens, New York, planned in 1909 by Frederick Law Olmstead, junior, and Grosvenor Atterbury, while further garden schemes were built in Britain and Europe in the years after the First World War.

But for many, the enduring dream of the Arts and Crafts movement remained the integration of the professional middle classes with village life, ideally through the rural craft guild. Ernest Gimson and Sidney Barnsley moved to Gloucestershire in 1893 because they felt that in the Cotswolds they could not only concentrate on their own ideas but also be inspired by rural life. Gimson later bought land at Sapperton with the intention of founding a community, but the First World War, and afterwards his own failing health, prevented this.

As an architect and designer, it was vital to Gimson not to be limited to the drawing-board, but to find firsthand experience of the materials and practical processes involved in building: this became synonymous with the mastery of disappearing craft techniques. In 1890 he had spent a few weeks learning the basic techniques of chair bodging from Philip Clissett, a traditional bodger from Herefordshire, who made turned, rush-seated chairs. He also spent time with a London firm of plasterworkers, and he continued to execute schemes of decorative plasterwork for ceilings, chimney-pieces, decorative friezes and even furniture, in which he was greatly influenced by examples of Elizabethan work. 'As regards design,' wrote Gimson in an essay on plasterwork, 'the first necessity is that the worker must show in his work something of the pleasure that he takes in natural things. And the second necessity is

appointed consulting architect in 1908. Baillie Scott again contributed to the project, with designs for flats for working women at Waterlow Court, a building of whitewashed brick with tiled roofs and a cloistered walkway around the garden. One of the prime movers in the Hampstead Garden Trust was Henrietta Barnet, wife of Canon S. A. Barnet, the first warden of Toynbee Hall and a founder of the Whitechapel Art Gallery.

The garden suburb idea spread to America, with projects such as Forest Hills Gar-

that he must have knowledge of old work, not that he may reproduce it, but that he may learn from it how to express his ideas. . . .' Gimson also returned to Tudor originals in the metalwork designs executed for him by Alfred Bucknell, the son of a local Cotswold blacksmith.

But it was in Sidney Barnsley's Cotswold work, perhaps more than in that of any other Arts and Crafts designer, that a true rural idiom was successfully re-employed. In his later work especially, Barnsley took the construction of agricultural tools and wagons as a basis; the wagon-back appeared in his designs for stretchers, and he adopted chamfering (used by wheelwrights to reduce the overall weight of a wagon without loss of strength) as a form of decoration. Gimson, too, adopted chamfering both as a reflection of traditional skills and as an attractive means of softening and enhancing the edges of his furniture.

Gimson and Sidney Barnsley were joined by Sidney's brother Ernest, and they and their families all became closely involved in village life, helping to revive the neglected traditions and revelries of the countryside. Their friend Alfred Powell described their rural life: 'It was wonderful [after] old smoky London to find yourself in those fresh clean rooms, furnished with good oak furniture and a trestle table that at seasonable hours surrendered its drawing-boards to a good English meal, in which figured, if I remember right, at least on guest nights, a great stone jar of best ale.' They made their own bread and cider, and cooked in a large brick oven which Philip Webb showed particular interest in. Another friend recalled Ernest Barnsley's search for authentic foods: 'A real

"bon viveur", he enjoyed not only eating a good dinner but buying the ingredients and cooking it himself, with his wife and daughters' assistance. Wherever he went he collected recipes for good dishes or the addresses from whence he could obtain special delicacies. His York hams and Wensleydale cheeses came from farms in Yorkshire direct, Welsh mutton from Brecon and pork pies from Melton Mowbray. . . . His sloe gin he made himself and loved to regale his many visitors on it.'

While the British enjoyed wallpaper and fabric patterns based on hedgerow flowers and foliage, and admired rustic pewter and rural oak, which seemed to symbolize an older, wiser England, other countries throughout the world, from Palestine to Finland, from Ireland to the Austro-Hungarian empire, found their own national symbolism through a revival of native decorative arts allied to folk traditions. In America, for example, a Harvard graduate, Charles F. Lummis, championed the cause of the American Indians, and there was a vogue for such indigenous crafts as Navajo blankets and Appalachian coverlets. In Russia, the Neo-Primitive painters Natalia Goncharova and her lifelong companion Mikhail Larionov, who turned their backs on Western art and embraced the culture and Byzantine religion of the East, were inspired by icons and the peasant woodcuts known as *lubki*.

In Norway, which was striving for independence from Sweden (the union was finally dissolved in 1905), there was a Viking revival: the heroic style and rich carving of such Viking forms as dragon heads appeared in furniture and silver. There was

'The Three Suitors', linen and wool tapestry designed in 1897 by Gerhard Munthe for the 1900 Exposition Universelle in Paris, and woven by Augusta Christensen at the Nordenfjeldske Kunstindustrimuseum Tapestry Studio, Trondheim. Museum für Kunst und Gewerbe, Hamburg

also a revival of weaving techniques. In 1897, the designer Frieda Hansen founded the Norwegian Tapestry Weaving Studio in Oslo producing large woven hangings with stylized flowers and motifs from Norwegian sagas, and the Norwegian Impressionist painter Gerhard Munthe exhibited tapestries based on Nordic legends at the Paris Exposition Universelle in 1900. Munthe also designed furniture painted and decorated with bold carvings of Nordic sagas and legends for a 'Fairy Tale Room' at the Holmenkollen Turisthotell in Oslo.

The Finns, too, turned to their ancient myths and legends as a means of asserting a sense of national identity. Finland had formed part of Sweden until 1809, when it fell under Russian domination as a grand duchy, but Swedish culture still held sway in Finnish society. While ordinary people had spoken Finnish for hundreds of years, the educated classes spoke Swedish, and many artists now returned to the Finnish language and to the movement known as Karelianism – the artistic expression of nationalism – named after the remote region in eastern Finland considered to be the source of the ancient dramatic epic, the *Kalevala*.

In 1890 the Finnish painter Akseli Gallen and the Swedish artist Count Louis Sparre went to Karelia in a romantic search for the inspirations of Finnish culture. They built a house there, named Kallela, near Ruovsi, in the style of the sturdy local log dwellings. At the Finnish pavilion at the Paris exhibition in 1900, Akseli Gallen exhibited examples of traditional *ryiji* textiles and Louis Sparre contributed the 'Iris Room', showing pottery, plain wooden furniture and metalwork from his Iris Workshops in Porvoo, Helsinki. Another exhibit was organized by the Friends of Finnish Handicrafts, an association founded in 1879 by Fanny Churberg with Morrisian ideals and the aim of preserving peasant traditions in embroidery and textiles. Similar associations were founded in emulation of the Friends in other Scandinavian countries.

The Finnish pavilion itself was designed by three architects, Eliel Saarinen, Herman Gesellius and Armas Lindgren, who had set up an office together in Helsinki in 1896. The inspiration of Karelianism was evident in an insurance company building they had designed in Helsinki with pine-cones around the windows and bears and squirrels guarding the entrance. In 1902, in emulation of Gallen and Sparre's Kallela, they created Hvitträsk, a group of buildings built

Interior of Hvitträsk, Finland, the log dwelling built by Eliel Saarinen, Herman Gesellius and Armas Lindgren in 1902–3

of rough stone and timber on a steep cliff overlooking the clear waters of Lake Hvitträsk; the place would house all three families and provide office and studio space. The interior had furniture carved with folk motifs, tiled hearths, decorated walls and embossed metalwork made by Erik Ehrström.

In Sweden itself, the expression of folk culture was less rugged and owed more to the elegant simplicity of the Gustavian revival, a style based on the houses built in and around Stockholm during the reign of King Gustav III of Sweden (1771–92). The best-known Swedish Arts and Crafts interiors were those created by the painter Carl Larsson and his wife Karin at their home in the Dalarna. Larsson, who had studied painting in Paris, depicted the interiors of their summer cottage in a series of light, unaffected watercolours published in a series of books: *Ett Hem* (A Home), 1899, *Larssons* (At The Larssons), 1902, and *Åt Solsiden* (On The Sunny Side), 1910. The abundant, clear colours of Karin Larsson's textiles and the painted Gustavian furniture in these unpretentious paintings of gardens and interiors were immensely popular. A German edition of *Åt Solsiden* was subtitled: 'A book about rooms to live in, about children, about you, about flowers, about everything.'

Throughout the countries under the yoke of either Russian or Austro-Hungarian rule – now Romania, Yugoslavia, Hungary, Czechoslovakia and Poland – artists, designers and architects embraced Arts and Crafts ideals, combining the modern forms of Art Nouveau with traditional folk culture in what became known as *Provinzkunst*. In Hungary for example, the 'Magyar' style of architecture of Ödön Lechner and Béla Lajta, which incorporated Transylvanian folk motifs, opposed the official styles of the Austro-Hungarian empire and reasserted both a link with the past and a sense of national identity. Empress Elizabeth, who had been created Queen of Hungary in 1867 in an attempt to placate Magyar nationalism, tactfully commissioned Ödön Faragó to make wooden furniture which combined both Art Nouveau and peasant motifs, and when Hungary celebrated its millennium in 1896, peasant costume and folk motifs were used to create a unifying theme even for official functions and occasions.

By the early years of this century, influenced by Ruskin and Tolstoy, Hungarian artists and architects such as the Young Ones group were using vernacular architecture and folk traditions to symbolize an ideal of closeness to nature, and in 1901 the Gödöllö artists' colony was established near Budapest, producing weaving, sculpture, leatherwork, stained glass and furniture. In 1906 at the Milan International Exposition they exhibited a furnished interior entitled 'The Home of the Artist' which showed a variety of influences from Britain, France and Austria. Walter Crane, whose work had been exhibited in Budapest, visited the colony and admired their work.

By 1900 Arts and Crafts ideals had become identified with political liberalism, with the rejection of the wealth and exploitation of the fast-growing cities and commercial centres, and with an unpretentious lifestyle that espoused a programme of traditional values, closeness to nature and a celebration of the mysticism of ancient myths and legends. It was – and remains – a potent mixture.

Watercolour of his own studio by Carl Larsson, from his book *Ett Hem*, published in Sweden in 1899. National Museum, Stockholm

C. F. A. VOYSEY

Charles Francis Annesley Voysey (1857–1941) was the son of a heretical clergyman from Yorkshire, and himself remained somewhat of a maverick, mistrustful of foreign influences and often difficult and inflexible with clients: like Philip Webb, he was prepared to turn down a commission rather than compromise. He was articled to the architect J. P. Seddon during the 1870s and set up his own practice in 1881, initially concentrating on decorative rather than architectural work. He joined the Art Workers' Guild in 1884 and was elected Master in 1924.

In 1883 his close friend A. H. Mackmurdo introduced him to Jeffrey and Co., for whom he began to design wallpapers; he went on to design for Turnbull and Stockdale and other wallpaper manufacturers, and from 1893 had a regular contract with Essex and Co.; from 1895 he was under contract to Alexander Morton to supply patterns for carpets and textiles. Voysey also designed tiles for Maw and Co., the Pilkington Tile and Pottery Co. and Minton's.

His favourite motifs were birds and trees, which he felt symbolized the joy of unspoilt nature and his own deeply-felt religious convictions. Swans, owls, seagulls, and flowers and foliage were depicted in simple, flat, stylized form.

He began designing furniture in the 1890s, showing a preference for pieces in plain oak decorated only with brass strap-hinges or his favourite pierced heart motif. Voysey felt that the horizontal signified repose, while the vertical represented vigour, and his furniture emphasizes structure and proportion, with tapering legs or supports which often end in a wide, square cap, an element borrowed from Mackmurdo. Between 1901 and 1914 most of his furniture was made by F. C. Nielson, although Liberty and Co. also made and sold his designs.

In 1899 Voysey built a house for himself, The Orchard, Chorleywood, from where he could commute to his architectural office via the newly-built Metropolitan Line – John Betjeman's 'Metro-land'. Nothing in his house, or in

Dining-room designed in 1902 by C.F.A. Voysey for a house in Birkenhead. The walls are panelled in oak and all the furniture was designed by Voysey and made by F.C. Nielson

the other four complete interiors he designed, was too small to win his attention, from the fire-tongs and door furniture to the clocks. The Orchard was plain and simple, with unadorned oak, white woodwork and whitewashed walls, green fireplace tiles, red curtains and green or patterned carpets. The only ornament, apart from the repeated heart motif, was a vase of flowers to leave one 'free as a bird to wander in the sunshine or storm of [one's] own thoughts'.

A home, Voysey believed, should have 'all the qualities of peace and rest and protection and family pride'. Outside, deep gables and long horizontal windows with mullions and leaded lights, porches and doors that were wide in proportion to their height, suggested shelter and welcome; inside, low ceilings and 'light, bright, cheerful rooms' were easy to clean and cheap to maintain. The servants' quarters, too, were bright and airy. His style was much copied here and in Europe.

'Let us Prey', textile design by C.F.A. Voysey. Victoria & Albert Museum, London

GIMSON AND THE BARNSLEYS

Ernest Gimson (1864–1919) was born in Leicester, the son of an engineer, and articled to a local architect. In January 1884 William Morris visited Leicester: Gimson and his brother met him at the station 'and, two minutes after his train had come in, we were at home with him and captured by his personality'. After his lecture on 'Art and Socialism', they all sat up talking. Morris later provided letters of introduction for Gimson to London architects, and, as a result, in 1886 he joined J. D. Sedding's office, next door to Morris and Co.'s Oxford Street showrooms, where he remained two years. Influenced by Morris, he joined the Society for the Protection of Ancient Buildings and the Art Workers' Guild.

In London Gimson met the Barnsley brothers, who came from a Nonconformist family of Birmingham builders. Ernest Barnsley (1863–1926) worked in Sedding's office, and Sidney (1865–1926) in Norman Shaw's. In October 1890, inspired by Morris and Co., Gimson and the Barnsleys along with W. R. Lethaby, Reginald Blomfield and Mervyn Macartney, also from Shaw's office and all members of the St George's Art Society, founded Kenton and Co., named after the street around the corner from their rented workshop in Bloomsbury.

They designed furniture for production by professional cabinet-makers. Although Gimson contributed a version of a traditional English dresser in unpolished chamfered oak, most of their pieces were influenced by the eighteenth-century originals admired by Shaw. Kenton and Co. furniture was used by Lethaby in two of his major decorating commissions, and exhibited at the premises of the Art Workers' Guild in 1891, but the firm closed the following year.

In 1893 Gimson and the Barnsleys moved out of London, intending to found a craft community with the aim of revitalizing traditional craftsmanship. They settled first at Ewen, near Circencester, then moved to Pinbury House, a run-down Elizabethan manor house, where they worked in the converted stables. In 1902 they moved again. Gimson and Ernest Barnsley went into partnership at Daneway House, employing cabinet-makers to produce furniture to their designs; Peter Waals, a Dutch cabinet-maker, became their foreman. The partnership foundered in 1905 and Barnsley returned to full-time architecture, but the workshops remained busy and successful, and by 1914 were employing more than a dozen men.

Although Gimson had studied turning and rushing, metalwork and forging, and decorative plasterwork, he made only a few early pieces of furniture himself, preferring to work closely with the craftsmen who executed his designs. He was a versatile designer, and made use of contrasting, geometric veneers as well as the solid woods favoured by Sidney Barnsley. Some of his work, such as the cabinets on stands with floral marquetry inlays, were inspired by Tudor pieces. After Gimson's death, the Daneway workshops closed and Waals opened his own workshop near Stroud.

Sidney Barnsley kept his own separate workshop at Sapperton in Gloucestershire, where he executed his own designs. He was basically self-taught. At first, he used English oak, neither polished nor stained, then other local woods, often obtained from the village wheelwright, such as ash, elm, deal and various fruitwoods, and finally English walnut and some imported woods. As he became more skilled, the heavier pieces such as coffers gave way to lighter, more varied work, constructed with open joinery and little superficial ornamentation, although he often made distinctive use of stringing (inlaid lines of alternate dark and light woods, usually ebony and holly). His work greatly influenced younger designers such as Ambrose Heal, Gordon Russell and A. Romney Green.

Right: Oak sideboard by Sidney Barnsley, 1924. Cheltenham Art Gallery and Museum; (*below left*) the interior of Ernest Barnsley's house, Daneway House, Sapperton in 1905 and (*below right*) a cabinet for storing fishing tackle, made of walnut with brass handles and decorative inlays of various fruitwoods, designed by Ernest Gimson in 1913

WALLPAPERS

'Bees' wallpaper designed by Candace Wheeler in 1881 and produced by
Warren, Fuller and Co., New York in 1882. Metropolitan Museum of
Art, New York
Opposite: 'Blue Fruit' wallpaper design by William Morris

The Victorian love of busy wallpaper patterns of 'cabbage roses and monster lilies' was replaced first by the flat patterns of Owen Jones and Pugin, then by the simple, conventionalized, floral patterns created by William Morris, and later by his assistant J. H. Dearle, or the stylized Anglo-Japanese designs of E. W. Godwin, Bruce Talbert or Christopher Dresser.

From 1864 Morris's wallpapers were produced for him by Jeffrey and Co., to whom Talbert, Walter Crane, Lewis F. Day and C. F. A. Voysey also supplied designs for papers, friezes, nursery papers and figurative panels. Many architects and artists – from A. H. Mackmurdo to Kate Greenaway – designed wallpapers.

Hand-blocked 'Art' papers, however, were expensive, and some people considered Morris's designs too large and palatial for ordinary homes. The order book for Watts and Co., founded in 1874 by the architects G. F. Bodley, Thomas Garner and George Gilbert Scott, junior, to make hand-blocked wallpapers in the Queen Anne revival style, was said to read like *Debrett*. The Silver Studio produced less expensive designs, and stencilling was even cheaper. In the 1890s 'Anaglypta', a lighter version of the embossed 'Lincrusta Walton' paper from the inventor of linoleum, Frederick Walton, was popular for dados.

By the late 1870s Morris and Co. wallpapers were widely available in America, and Christian Herter, L. C. Tiffany and Samuel Coleman all designed Japanese-inspired papers. In 1881, when the New York firm, Warren, Fuller and Co., held a competition for designs, Candace Wheeler, her daughter Dora, and her friends Ida Clark and Caroline Townsend who had become members of Associated Artists, won all four prizes. They continued to supply designs which were increasingly based on American themes.

In Europe, Hector Guimard was among those creating Art Nouveau patterns, but gradually a lighter style prevailed. Otto Eckmann supplied stylized designs for the Mannheim firm, Engelhardt, while in Austria the geometric designs of Josef Hoffmann were gradually replaced by the more baroque, folk-inspired style of Dagobert Peche and Mathilde Flögl. By the 1920s patterned wallpaper was considered positively Victorian and had been replaced in modern homes by whitewashed walls.

Left: Designs for wallpapers by Alphonse Mucha, 1902. Victoria & Albert Museum, London

Opposite: Hand-knotted 'Hammersmith' carpet by William Morris, *c.*1880

CARPETS

'Lily', the popular machine-woven wool pile carpet designed by William Morris c.1875 and manufactured by the Wilton Royal Carpet Factory; and (*opposite*) a carpet designed by C.F.A. Voysey

The design of carpets, like that of other flat patterns for wallpapers and textiles, rejected the naturalistic, three-dimensional effects that had reigned supreme at the Great Exhibition of 1851 in favour of conventionalized designs that would give no impression of depth or shading. Owen Jones, Digby Wyatt and Pugin all led the change in taste, but, as with so much, it was William Morris who created the most satisfying designs, based on oriental traditions but using larger areas of simple colour.

Morris became interested in Persian carpets in the 1870s, and in 1878 he made his first hand-tufted carpet on a loom in the back attic at Queen Square. The loom was then moved to the coach-house at Hammersmith and, in 1881, to the Merton Abbey works, but these hand-knotted rugs, made with naturally-dyed wools, were always known as Hammersmith carpets. They were extremely expensive, and the larger ones, such as one for George Howard's house, Naworth, took nearly a year to complete.

Influenced by Morris, in 1898 James Morton of the Carlisle carpet and textile firm Alexander Morton and Co., set up the first of three factories in Ireland producing hand-woven Donegal carpets, which were sold through Liberty and Co., Morton's main English agent. (Morton's machine-made carpets included bold, stylized floral designs by C. F. A. Voysey and Lindsay Butterfield.)

Hand-woven Kildare carpets, dyed with natural native dyes, were also produced in Ireland at a firm founded in 1903 with the support of the Countess of Mayo. These rugs were plain with decorative borders.

Morris's designs for machine-woven rugs and carpets, with small motifs in dark, practical colours, were made for the firm by the Wilton Royal Carpet Factory and the Heckmondwike Manufacturing Co. in Yorkshire. In America, old-established manufacturers such as the Bigelow Carpet Co. of Clinton, Massachusetts, produced machine-woven Wiltons in fashionable Arts and Crafts designs.

METALWORK

Metalwork designed by C.F.A. Voysey and made by W. Bainbridge
Reynolds's metalworking firm, c.1896–1903 and (*opposite*) a cast iron
fireplace by Thomas Jekyll

Fireplaces and fire-irons, door and window furniture, decorative hinges and handles for furniture, and larger architectural features all received attention from designers and architects. Items such as doorplates or firedogs with the handmade beaten or hammered appearance, first made popular by the metalworkers of Ashbee's Guild of Handicraft, became an essential component of the Arts and Crafts interior.

During the rage for all things Aesthetic, sunflowers, chrysanthemums and other Japanese motifs appeared on the cast-iron fire grates designed by Thomas Jekyll in the 1870s or on the brass door furniture produced by firms such as the Nashua Lock Co. of New Hampshire, in America.

In 1903 the architect Ernest Gimson established Alfred Bucknell, the son of a local blacksmith, in his own smithy at Sapperton in Gloucestershire: he was eventually assisted by three men, making firedogs, handles, locks, window latches, candlesticks and other items in iron, brass, polished steel and silver to Gimson's designs. Bucknell learned

many of his techniques by copying original Elizabethan examples. In Philadelphia, the Polish immigrant Samuel Yellin based his work on medieval originals.

Voysey designed a wide range of metalwork, including bolts, window catches, letter-boxes, keyhole covers and door handles, which incorporated motifs such as birds or hearts. In 1912 Harry Peach, of Dryad Handicrafts, went into partnership with William Pick, who ran the Leicestershire Art metalwork firm of Collins and Co., to make door furniture, fire-irons and fenders in the Arts and Crafts style, as well as bronze candlesticks, silver tea-sets and even jewellery.

Among the architects who made bold use of decorative ironwork were Antoni Gaudi in Barcelona, Louis Sullivan in Chicago, Hector Guimard in France (his Art Nouveau railings still adorn the Paris Métro), and Charles Rennie Mackintosh, who used cast-iron features to add an heraldic éclat to both the interior and exterior of Glasgow School of Art.

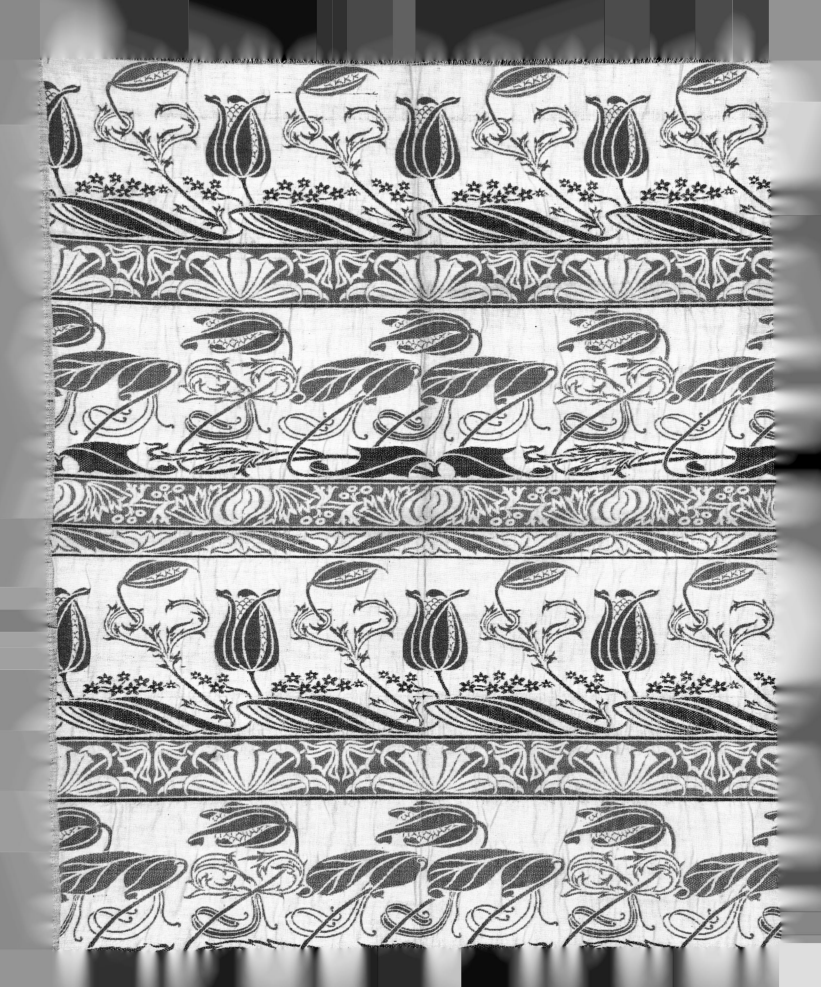

A Middle-Class Enthusiasm

The Arts and Crafts movement provided a new middle-class fashion for interior decoration, and few suburban homes were without their panel of stained glass, their beaten metal vase or carefully displayed piece of 'studio' pottery from Doulton's Art Pottery, Moorcroft, Pilkington's Lancastrian or, in America, Rookwood, Fulper or Grueby. Those who could not afford an architect-designed house could, and did, purchase 'Art' furniture, wallpapers, nursery friezes, rugs or tea-sets in order to display their modernity. The enthusiasm for Art furnishings in England diminished only with the outbreak of war in 1914, and in America continued on into the 1920s.

In America especially, economic expansion and the growth of both manufacturing and service industries in the decades following the Civil War had created a huge middle class: the aspirations of this growing army of salesmen, managers and office workers were chronicled by writers such as Theodore Dreiser who sensed the loss of autonomy experienced by many of the small cogs in the great machine that seemed to benefit only the likes of Carnegie, Morgan or Rockefeller. The chance to participate in an art movement that defied industrialism and upheld the sanctity of individual expression was extremely appealing to the new class of wage-slaves. Enthusiasts for the new style could not only buy work by William Morris or Walter Crane in their local department stores, and read about the latest designs in magazines such as *The Studio* or *Country Life* in England or *The Ladies' Home Journal* or *House & Garden* in America, but could also join Arts and Crafts societies or attend craft classes.

As Walter Crane wrote in 1887, by which time he had become a committed socialist: 'There is room for the highest qualities in the pattern of a carpet, the design of a wallpaper, a bit of repoussé or wrought iron or wood carving. The sincere designer and craftsman . . . with his invention and skill applied to the accessories of everyday life may do more to keep alive the sense of beauty than the greatest painter that ever lived.' Those who flocked to learn embroidery, china-painting or wood-carving could believe that they were joining ranks with the artists they admired.

The leading English designers were well-known in both Europe and America, thanks to the numerous international exhibitions at which British decorative arts took pride of place, and English wallpapers, textiles and ceramics were also successfully

Silk and cotton woven textile, possibly designed by Archibald Knox for the Silver Studios, *c.*1899. Victoria & Albert Museum, London

Bedroom furniture illustrated in a Liberty and Co. catalogue of 1890

several such 'curio' shops selling Indian silks, Chinese porcelain, oriental rugs and 'Arabian' furniture. But gradually Liberty began to see the potential in the craze for Art furnishings, and in 1883 he opened a furnishing and decoration studio under the management of Leonard F. Wyburd. Liberty was astute enough not only to create his own version of Arts and Crafts but to buy designs from most of the leading artists. The Liberty style, however, both popularized and trivialized the movement, turning Ruskin and Morris's ideals of 'honest craftsmanship' and freedom of expression into a mere fad of fashion, albeit an extremely successful one.

Most of Liberty's own furniture, including the 'Thebes' stool, was designed by Wyburd, and in 1887 Liberty's established their own cabinet-making workshops, producing simple chairs and country-style oak furniture with inlaid decoration, inset tiles (sometimes by de Morgan), leaded-glass panels and elaborate strap-hinges and metal handles. In later years, some of their bedroom suites were given Saxon names such as 'Helga', 'Ethelwynn' and 'Athelstan' to reinforce their self-consciously 'quaint' character. 'Athelstan', which was sold from 1902 until 1911, included dressing-tables, chairs, tables, chests of drawers, wardrobes of various sizes with hand-stained panels of landscape designs, and beds in oak with the pierced heart motif beloved by Voysey, but these suites were cumbersome and exaggerated, and lacked the sophistication of the prototypes by Mackmurdo, Baillie Scott or Voysey on which they were modelled.

Liberty's, however, also stocked furniture from outside manufacturers and designers, including a line of eighty-one pieces of

exported. One of the most influential of the European shops was the Maison de l'Art Nouveau, opened in Paris in 1895 by the Hamburg dealer Siegfried (later changed to Samuel) Bing: L. C. Tiffany, John La Farge, Henri van de Velde, W. A. S. Benson and Frank Brangwyn were among some of the artists and designers associated with the gallery.

But the most important retail outlet of all was one which, in Italy, gave its name to the style it inspired – *Stile Liberty*. Liberty and Co. was founded in Regent Street, London, in 1875 by Arthur Lasenby Liberty, a former manager of Farmer and Roger's 'oriental' department, where Godwin, Rossetti and Whistler had purchased their Japanese prints. Several of the new department stores, including Whiteleys and Debenham and Freebody, had opened oriental departments, and Liberty's was at first only one of

Original examples introduced by Liberty & Co. in practical shapes,
made and decorated by hand. The surface of this beautiful
pottery is enriched with lustrous and scintillating glazes.

No. 1.
6 ins. diameter.
14/6

No. 2.
4 ins. high.
10/6

No. 3.
6 ins. diameter.
9/3

No. 4.
6 ins. high, 6/9
9½ ,,   16/6

No. 5.
6 ins. high.
5/-

No. 6.
11 ins. diameter.
18/6

No. 7.
7½ ins. high.
12/9

No. 8.
6 ins. diameter, 6/6
7   ,,   7/6
8¼ ,,   9/6

No. 9.
9 ins. high.
17/6

No. 10.
8 ins. high.
15/6

No. 11.
11½ ins. high.
£1 2 6

No. 12.
9 ins. high.
9/6

Silver mirror frame designed by Archibald Knox in 1902 for Liberty's 'Cymric' range. Virginia Museum of Fine Arts

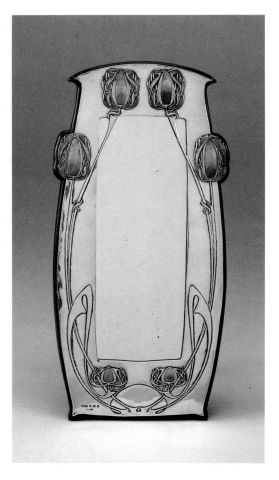

furniture designed by Baillie Scott and made at John P. White's Pyghtle Works in Bedford; there were also designs by Voysey and by George Walton, whose furniture was made by William Birch and, later, E. G. Punnett, of High Wycombe.

Baillie Scott had begun contributing fabric designs to Liberty and Co. in 1893; Walter Crane, the Scots illustrator Jessie M. King, and Voysey were also among those who sold designs and were prepared to accept Liberty's strict rule on anonymity.

Many of Liberty's fabrics were printed by William Morris's early associate, Thomas Wardle, who also supplied the store with imported Indian silks (which he dyed and printed at his works in Leek), and with printed cottons, and silks for embroidery. The most famous Liberty Art fabrics came from the Silver Studio, even though the majority of the studio's pattern designs were in fact bought by French manufacturers. The Silver Studio was founded in 1880 by the textile designer Arthur Silver, and after his death in 1896 was managed by his son Rex, who designed for Liberty's 'Cymric' and 'Tudric' metalwork ranges. Harry Napper became design manager for a couple of years before leaving to work freelance.

Arthur Liberty was little concerned with the issues that concerned Morris or Ashbee about hand-craftsmanship or the working conditions of the craftsman, and his successful policy of buying designs by good, modern designers and having them made up by established manufacturers seriously undercut the craft workshops. Ashbee bitterly blamed the competition from Liberty metalwork for the failure of his Guild. Nevertheless, many small firms relied on Liberty's success as a retailer: several of the new Art potteries such as Bretby, Brannam, Della Robbia, Moorcroft and Pilkington's Lancastrian, and, later, Doulton and Wedgwood, all sold their wares through the store.

One of Liberty's own most successful ventures was the launch in 1899 of their range of handmade 'Cymric' gold and silverware, mostly made by the Birmingham firm of W. H. Haseler. A second line of pewter wares, named 'Tudric' followed the next year. Several designers were involved in the project, including Jessie M. King, Rex Silver, Arthur Gaskin and Bernard Cuzner, producing designs for a wide range of jewellery, cigarette cases, jewellery boxes, tea-sets, jugs, vases, candlesticks, mirror frames and clocks. Some of it was decorated with elegant turquoise enamelwork. The most distinctive designs, which formed the basis of Liberty's popular and influential 'Celtic Revival', were by Archibald Knox.

The son of a marine engineer, Knox was a Manxman who was deeply interested in the island's Celtic traditions and had made a study of Celtic ornament. He was probably first introduced to Liberty and Co. by Baillie Scott, whom he had met at the Art School in Douglas, and in whose office he had worked for a time. Probably at Baillie Scott's suggestion, he began to send designs for fabrics and wallpapers to Liberty's around 1895 and continued to contribute designs for metalwork, jewellery, carpets and garden ornaments for several years. Knox's distinctive Celtic designs for the 'Cymric' and 'Tudric' lines were widely admired and imitated. He never merely copied existing forms: since his boyhood, he had perfected his own, far from simple versions of Celtic scripts and *entrelac* designs, and much of the superbly controlled delicacy and intricacy of his own Celtic lettering echoed the sinuous, organic style of Art Nouveau.

Among the many other shops and manufacturers that tried to emulate Liberty's success in selling Art furnishings was John Sollie Henry, who produced elegant pieces of Georgian-style furniture inlaid with pretty, stylized motifs of stained wood or metal. In an advertisement of 1896, he

Oak buffet with repoussé copper panel, gilt inlay and gilt wrought iron hinges and lock plates, designed by M.H. Baillie Scott

described himself as a 'Designer of Quaint and Artistic Furniture'. W. A. S. Benson, who had introduced a similar refinement to Morris and Co.'s furnishings after Morris's death, also designed for J. S. Henry, whose delicate chairs, desks and cabinets were well suited to the lighter style of the Queen Anne revival.

In America, perhaps the most quaint and eccentric of the Arts and Crafts designers was Charles Rohlfs. He was the only American cabinet-maker invited to exhibit at the Turin International Exhibition of 1902, and he received commissions from the crowned heads of both Great Britain and Italy as well as from many other wealthy clients. Rohlfs was born in New York, the son of a cabinet-maker, who died when he was only twelve years old. He served his apprenticeship at a foundry, while attending evening classes at the Cooper Union, in the hope of becoming an actor, then found work designing cast-iron stoves and furnaces. He was past his mid-thirties when, around 1889, he began to design and make elaborately pierced and carved oak Gothic furniture in his own workshop in Buffalo. Friends commissioned pieces, and gradually his fame grew. By 1909 he still worked out of the same workshop, but employed eight artisans to execute his designs.

His dark, sturdy chairs, chests and desks are unique: not quite Gothic, not quite Moorish, not quite in the traditions of Scandinavian carved furniture, yet distinctly belonging to the decade that produced Art Nouveau. In 1907 Rohlfs himself described his work as 'strangely suggestive of the days when the world was young, but in spite of that, distinctive of this progressive twentieth century and strictly American. It has the spirit of today blended with the poetry of medieval ages.'

Throughout Britain, Europe and America the desire for beauty in the home led to the foundation of numerous 'studio' potteries and glassworks. Many were founded by individual artist-potters who were searching for some elusive technique, finish or glaze effect. William de Morgan's lustre experiments come to mind in this connection, as do the attractive decorative bowls and plaques made in emulation of Italian originals at Harold Rathbone's Della Robbia Company, founded in Birkenhead in 1894. There were also W. Howson Taylor's attempts to achieve the deep-red Chinese *sang de boeuf* high-fired glazes at the Ruskin Pottery, established in Birmingham in 1898 and the distinctive crackled metallic finishes which Sir Edmund Elton developed around 1900 at the Sunflower Pottery on his family's Somerset estate.

The success of these individual artist-potters led the commercial potteries to set up their own 'studio' departments. Firms such as the Worcester Royal Porcelain Co., Minton's or Wedgwood had responded quickly to the vogue for Japanese-inspired wares. Doulton and Co. then opened a factory for studio pots at Lambeth, where artists such as Hannah Barlow and George Tinworth produced distinctive work, while Wedgwood produced a small number of vases and bowls designed by Lindsay Butterfield and known as 'Lindsay Ware'.

In 1875 Wedgwood had brought Thomas Allen from Minton's to be director of their Fine Art Studios, where he remained until 1904. His portrait plaques and pseudo-historical subjects, such as the 'Ivanhoe' series, were similar to the wide range of quaint illustrated wares later produced by Doulton and Co., and were typical of the Edwardian interpretation of the romantic and chivalric themes featured by Morris in his poetry and by Burne-Jones in his art. Similar subjects were depicted, with greater originality, by Walter Crane, Lewis F. Day and C. F. A. Voysey in their designs for Pilkington's Lancastrian wares. A final flowering of the fey sweetness that came to be associated with Arts and Crafts images was Daisy Makeig-Jones's 'Fairyland Lustre', first produced by Wedgwood in 1915.

In America, too, Art potteries sprang up all over the country. Some individuals, such as Louise McLaughlin or Maria Longworth Nichols, who founded Rookwood, were inspired by the examples of French or Japanese ceramics they had seen at the Philadelphia Centennial Exposition. Some firms, such as the J. and J. G. Low Art Tile Works

Mahogany display cabinet inlaid with various woods and made by J.S. Henry and Co. in 1904

in Chelsea, Massachusetts, began to produce architectural and decorative tiles in imitation of English originals, having recognized the demand that there would be for such products. One of the most distinctive forms of American ceramics was produced by William H. Grueby, who had been employed at the Lows' Art Tile Works before opening his own pottery in Boston in 1894. Grueby produced vases of thick, moulded organic shapes with a heavy matt glaze, usually green, enhanced with yellow or blue, which was widely copied. In Colorado, Artus van Briggle, who had worked at Rookwood, also used matt glazes with sculptural Art Nouveau forms. At the Fulper Pottery, New Jersey, in 1909 the grandson of the founder began producing a range of Art pottery called 'Vase-Kraft' in a variety of matt, flambé, lustre and crystalline glazes. Other individuals who experimented with different glaze effects were Ernest A. Batchelder, Charles Volkmar and Frederick Hurten Rhead.

As early as the 1870s Morris had complained of being tired of 'ministering to the swinish luxury of the rich' and began to long for greater simplicity, but by the time of his death in 1896 the success of the style he had created had taken on a commercial life of its own. Although A. H. Mackmurdo later wrote that the Arts and Crafts movement had been 'a mighty upheaval of man's spiritual nature', many liberal, well-meaning Arts and Crafts designers found themselves unable to do more than produce Art furniture for the newly liberalized middle classes, revolutionizing the middle-class home but not the lives of the working people who produced it.

Opposite: Oak fall-front desk by Charles Rohlfs, decorated with brass nailheads and hammered surface texture, 1898–1901; the whole desk revolves upon its base. Virginia Museum of Fine Arts

Left: Earthenware vase decorated with white jonquils, designed by Wilhelmina Post and produced at the Grueby Faience Co. in Massachusetts

LIGHTING

Thomas Alva Edison developed the first practical model of the incandescent filament bulb in October 1879, and thenceforward designers could dispense with the requirements of bulky oil reservoirs, gas pipes and the hazards of naked flames. In his 'Notes on Electric Wiring and Fittings', written in 1887, W. A. S. Benson, who considered artificial lighting to be a 'fine art', discussed not only the different uses of light in different rooms but also the artistic effects that could be achieved. In 1896 the *Magazine of Art* called his designs 'palpitatingly modern'.

Benson, who interpreted the requirements of electric light in an inventive and technically ingenious way, was a close friend of Burne-Jones and a co-founder of the Art Workers' Guild. As a boy, he had been taught the use of lathes and machinery by his uncle, an amateur scientist and craftsman. He was then articled to the architect Basil Champneys and set up in business as a designer in London in 1880. His catalogue for 1899–1900 lists over eight hundred items, other than electric light fittings, made of copper, brass, iron, polished steel, electroplate and silver, and includes firescreens, trays, teapots, electric kettles and vacuum flasks as well as oil lamps, candlesticks and reflective candle sconces. His wares were often finished with bronzing, lacquer or with dark grey or other coloured films. Veined vaseline, ruby, olive green or opalescent glass shades were provided by Powell's of Whitefriars.

In America and Europe, the development of electric light coincided with the rise of Art Nouveau. Natural forms, especially flowers, were used for lamps, with the stem disguising the wires and the drooping petals forming shades that could now safely enclose the light source. Lights with L. C. Tiffany's leaded-glass shades, or the lamps of carved cameo glass by Emile Gallé or Daum Frères, could glow romantically in dark corners. Tiffany soon had his imitators: the Steuben Glass Works and the Quezal Art Glass and Decorating Co. also made elaborate glass lampshades.

At his San Francisco workshop, Dirk van Erp combined hammered copper bases with shades made of strong, trans-

Green-glazed pottery lamp with inset pink and green glass, made by the Fulper Pottery Company of New Jersey, *c.*1910 (Virginia Museum of Fine Arts) and (*opposite*) a dining room showing a copper chandelier designed by W.A.S. Benson, with candlesticks possibly designed by Giles Gilbert Scott and wall-mounted lights by Ernest Gimson. Private collection, Birkenhead

lucent mica – clear, yellow or amber – to veil the bright electric light. Gustav Stickley and the Roycroft shops both produced plain wooden lamps in keeping with the Craftsman style; Frank Lloyd Wright also designed wooden lamps as part of his overall decorative schemes. At the Wiener Werkstätte, the simplicity of Josef Hoffmann's designs for electric light fittings began to show a truly modern awareness of the demands of the new technology.

The old forms of lighting did not immediately give way to electricity, however, and candles especially continued to be used, even if only for the beauty of their flames. In Chicago, for example, the Scottish-born Robert Riddle Jarvie, a friend of George Grant Elmslie, made candlesticks and lanterns in brass, copper or patinated bronze.

Right: Hammered copper lamp with mica shade from Dirk van Erp's San Francisco workshop, *c.*1919

Opposite: 'Lotus' leaded glass table lamp on a bronze base, by Tiffany Studios

THE HOSPITABLE BOARD

Domestic wares produced by Doulton, Wedgwood, Moorcroft, the Poole Pottery, the Martin Brothers and Liberty and Co, from 1874 to 1930, including a coffee pot designed for Doulton by Frank Brangwyn, a Liberty and Co. 'Tudric' clock and a plate from Wedgwood's 'Ivanhoe' series. Private collection

Ladies wore high-waisted Aesthetic tea-gowns in pale, muted shades, amber beads around their necks. Seated before an ebonized Godwin table, they poured tea from silver or electroplated tea-sets by Dresser or Benson, or from the fashionable rustic pewter of Liberty's 'Tudric' range, and offered hot scones from a Guild of Handicraft handmade silver muffin dish.

In Denmark, Georg Jensen, who had been apprenticed to a goldsmith before studying sculpture, opened his own workshop in Copenhagen in 1904, and was assisted from 1906 by Johan Rohde and later by several other goldsmiths and designers. He produced robust, naturalistic tablewares in silver, often decorated with roses or fruit.

Plain, sturdy glasses might be designed by Philip Webb for Powell's of Whitefriars, while, in Europe in the first decade of this century, Richard Riemerschmid and Peter Behrens designed glassware for Benedikt von Poschinger in Oberzweiselau, and the Wiener Werkstätte produced pretty wineglasses and decanters decorated with black or coloured enamels as well as a wide range of metalwork and ceramics.

There was a vast range of ceramics available, from the delicate Japanese-inspired porcelains produced by Royal Worcester to the unpretentious painted and lustre decorations by Alfred Powell for Wedgwood tablewares, first exhibited in 1905. Powell and his wife Louise were friends and neighbours of Gimson and the Barnsleys, and Sidney Barnsley's daughter Grace also worked with them. In Germany, Henri van de Velde and Riemerschmid designed tea-sets and dinner-services for the venerable Meissen factory, while in Sweden around the turn of the century the painter Gunnar Wennerberg introduced simple designs based upon such wild flowers as snowdrops, cowslips and lilies-of-the-valley to the Gustavsberg ceramics factory.

TILES

Tiles by William de Morgan in a bathroom at 8 Addison Road, Holland Park, and (*opposite*) a collection of tiles by Minton's (the 'Four Seasons' and the 'Wolf and the Crane'), W.B. Simpson and Sons (central panel), William de Morgan (flower designs) and Wedgwood (blue and white tiles)

Hand-made encaustic floor tiles – usually consisting of red-brown clay moulds, filled in with clays of different colours to form designs based on medieval originals – were produced from the 1830s by Minton and Co. of Stoke-on-Trent and Chamberlain's Worcester, a firm, which in the 1850s moved to Shropshire and became Maw and Co.

The Dutch technique of making hand-painted, tin-glazed earthenware Delft tiles, which were too delicate to be used on the floor, gave way to mass production after the development of transfer printing. But the tiles decorated by William de Morgan and those associated with Morris and Co. revived the art of hand-painting. The housing boom of the 1880s and 1890s led to an increased demand for tiles, which, because they were hygienic and easily washable, were popular for dairies, butchers' shops, hospitals, museums, railway stations, pubs and hotels, as well as for the bathrooms, kitchens, fireplaces and entrance halls of suburban houses. Around 1900 the dust-pressing process began to be used to make relief-moulded tiles in fashionable Art Nouveau styles.

Maw and Co., the Pilkington Tile and Pottery Co., and Minton's were the leading British manufacturers, and Walter Crane, Lewis F. Day, Moyr Smith and C. F. A. Voysey were among the many artists who designed for them. Their subject-matter varied from simple animal or floral designs to illustrations from Aesop, Walter Scott or Shakespeare.

In America, at least fifty tile companies were founded between 1875 and 1920; among these were the American Encaustic Tiling Co. of Zanesville, Ohio, who reproduced designs by Crane and other English designers; the J. and J. G. Low Art Tile Works who made moulded, glazed tiles with Japanese-inspired designs of birds, fans and small geometric patterns; the Grueby Faience Co. whose matt glazes came to dominate the market; and the Chelsea Keramik Art Works near Boston which also produced Art tiles that could be inset in furniture or even framed. In 1877 a dozen leading artists including Augustus St Gaudens and Winslow Homer went so far as to found a Tile Club in New York; this was entirely devoted to painting tiles.

THE NURSERY

'Afternoon Tea' by Kate Greenaway, from the *Girl's Own Paper*, 1887

The 1890s ushered in a golden age of childhood. In contrast to the mid-century, it was now believed that a child's sensitivity and intuition were strongly influenced by its environment, and the nursery had to be the brightest, sunniest room in the house. As early as 1874 E. W. Godwin's children had worn tiny kimonos, and their mother, Ellen Terry, later related how '. . . they were allowed no rubbishy picture books, but from the first Japanese prints and fans lined their nursery walls and Walter Crane was their classic. If injudicious friends gave them the wrong sort of present, it was promptly burned! . . . a mechanical mouse . . . was taken away as being realistic and common. Only wooden toys were allowed.'

Fanciful fairy-tales and whimsical folklore were encouraged, and many illustrators of children's books designed decorative nursery friezes, wallpapers, fireside rugs and chintzes for commercial manufacturers, or saw their work widely imitated. Leading architects and designers also produced plans for nurseries, sometimes when their own families were small. In 1912, for example, Jessie M. King designed an elegant and imaginative white-painted nursery complete with stained-glass panels, cupboards decorated with scenes from 'The Frog Prince' and a specially designed doll's house and rocking-horse.

Before the twentieth century was ten years old, stores such as Liberty's, Heal's, and Story and Co. of Kensington were producing entire suites of nursery furniture. The small size of the various items, which were often fancifully decorated, coloured or shaped, showed a new sensitivity to a child's needs and feelings.

Around 1900 the alphabets, maxims, morals and biblical sayings of earlier nursery crockery gave way to more whimsical, less didactic designs, and the Edwardian celebration of Christmas no doubt enlived the gift-set market. Doulton's earliest wares feature such subjects as mermaids, medieval legends, and games and pastimes such as children tobogganing, all rendered in quite sophisticated styles.

By the 1920s all the major manufacturers – Doulton, Wedgwood, Shelley, Paragon – were producing nursery wares decorated with anthropomorphized animals or scenes from nursery rhymes and contemporary children's books. Mabel Lucie Atwell, for example, designed for Shelley, while Randolph Caldecott had contributed to Doulton's nursery wares as early as 1882.

From 1890, to Burne-Jones's delight, drawing was taught in all elementary schools, and in 1897 the Educational Handwork Association was founded to urge handcraft teaching for older children. The new educational theories put forward by Franz Cizek in Vienna, or Maria Montessori in Rome, endorsed the creative activity and self-expression earlier advocated by J. H. Pestalozzi or Friedrich Froebel. Towards the end of the First World War, Harry Peach developed Dryad Handicrafts, supplying felt, wooden beads and materials for weaving, vegetable dyeing or linoleum printing which were used not only by children but also as occupational therapy for wounded soldiers.

The heyday of Peter Pan, however, was short-lived: ironically, in the 1920s, while manufacturers continued to develop the flourishing market in children's wares, attitudes to childhood and childcare hardened. By 1934 *The Daily Express Book of Home Management* could conclude that 'one of the most important items of nursery furniture is the clock'!

Right: Doll's house of painted wood designed by Jessie M. King as part of a nursery, exhibited *c.*1912. Victoria & Albert Museum, London

Below: Chintz based on the nursery rhyme *The House that Jack Built*, designed by C.F.A. Voysey in 1929 and sold to Morton Sundour

Opposite: Selection of nursery wares from the early 1920s: a duck bowl from the Ashstead Pottery, a cup and saucer painted by Stella Crofts, a mug painted by Jessie M. King and a ship bowl painted by Annie Macbeth, a student from the Glasgow School of Art

ILLUSTRATORS

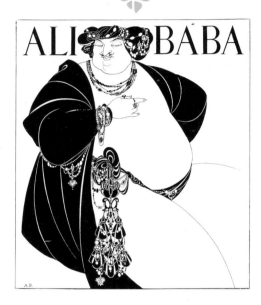

Cover design by Aubrey
Beardsley for a proposed
edition of *The Forty
Thieves*, 1897. Fogg Art
Museum, Massachusetts

The new wave of children's literature was illustrated by a new generation of artists – Beatrix Potter, Edmund Dulac, Arthur Rackham, Jessie M. King, Kate Greenaway and Walter Crane – many of whom, even in their 'adult' work, appealed to the child within.

The young Walter Crane was already working as an illustrator when, in 1867, a naval friend returned from Japan with a collection of Japanese prints. When he subsequently met William Morris, Crane's work went on to combine the simplified colours and flat, stylized manner of Japanese art with the romantic themes of Morris and Burne-Jones. Between 1870 and 1874 he produced more than twenty 'toy' books, including old fairy-tales, rhymes and pictorial ABCs, for Edward Evans of Routledge and Evans, the publisher who first exploited the revolution in colour printing processes. Crane has been described by Maurice Sendak as an 'ornamental illustrator', and many of his illustrations depicted blue and white tiles, sunflowers, peacock feathers and Japanese fans. By 1875 his skills were in demand among architects and manufacturers who wanted decorative designs for wallpapers, friezes, textiles and tiles.

But in 1878 Crane's success was eclipsed by Kate Greenaway's first book for Routledge and Evans, *Under The Window*. She had been designing Christmas cards for ten years, when her father, an engraver, introduced her to Evans. Her demure, Aesthetic children, dressed in their Queen Anne revival outfits proved extremely popular: even Ruskin sent her letters of admiration. She wrote her own poems as well as illustrating well-known rhymes and tales.

Evans's third success was with Randolph Caldecott, who produced fourteen books between 1878 and his early death in 1886. His style was more boisterous and realistic than either Crane's or Greenaway's.

For adults, however, there was a darker side to the new illustrators. Charles Ricketts and Charles Shannon incorporated the sinuous lines of continental Art Nouveau into their work, while in April 1894 the publisher John Lane launched *The Yellow Book* with Aubrey Beardsley as art editor. Both Ricketts and Beardsley illustrated work by Oscar Wilde, making the most of the decadent, erotic language of such plays as *Salomé*.

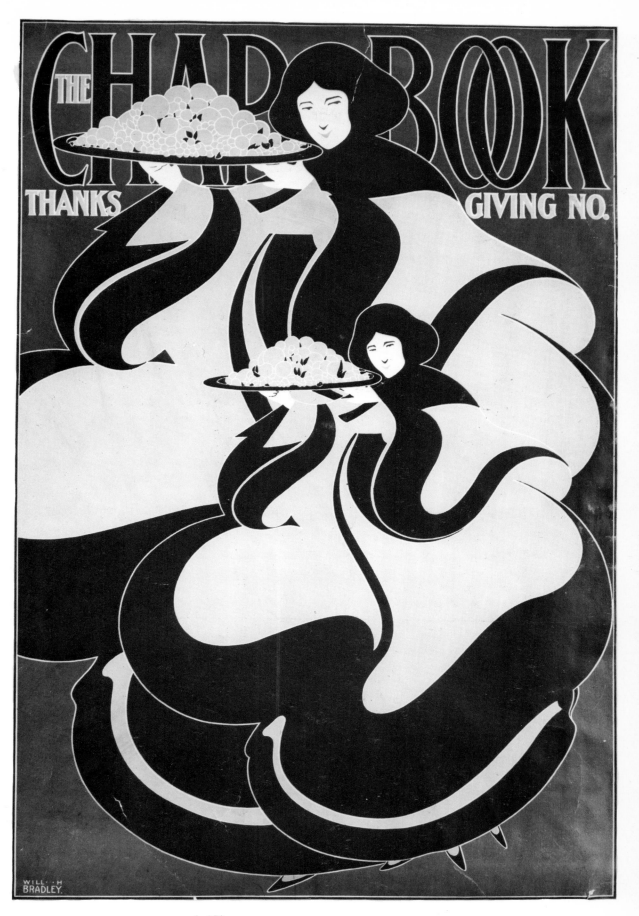

Cover for Stone and Kimball's *Chap-Book*, 1894, by Will Bradley, an American graphic artist best known for his work for periodicals and commercial posters

The Benediction
of Good Taste

Woman's place has never lain more repressively within the home than in the 1860s and 1870s. Women became the guardian angels of the hearth, the upholders of the sacred values of the Victorian home, safely protected from contamination by the outside world. Never had social convention made it more difficult for women to escape the restraints laid upon them in the name of modesty and womanliness.

William Morris, the first to do away with so many conventions, not only married out of his class – Janey Burden was the daughter of an Oxford stableman, Morris financially independent – but also encouraged his wife, sister-in-law and not a few of the other women associated with the firm, such as Kate and Lucy Faulkner, the sisters of his friend Charles Faulkner, to become involved in its work, designing and executing tile-painting, gesso work, wallpaper and, above all, embroidery. Morris himself was not completely without his own ideal of womanhood, and embroidery exemplified his treasured image of the medieval damozel at work upon the hangings for her castle bedchamber. He himself first become interested in embroidery when decorating the Red House, and it subsequently became a vital part of Morris and Co.'s range. Janey

Morris, her sister Elizabeth Burden, Catherine Holiday, wife of the painter and stained glass designer Henry Holiday, Madeleine Wardle, wife of the firm's business manager and, later, Morris's daughter May, all executed designs by Morris, Burne-Jones and others.

The decorative arts were thought to be admirably suited to women, not only because they were associated with the adornment of the home but also because by their very nature – painstaking, delicate, refined – such arts were considered suitably 'feminine'. The Aesthetic movement, which preached that beautiful surroundings promoted spiritual and mental health, made it even more fashionable for women to involve themselves directly in the decoration of their homes; a display of exquisite taste became as important as dressing well and looking beautiful. Both Doulton's and Minton's supplied blank tiles for fashionable young ladies to decorate, and Morris and Co. sold not only finished embroidery work, but also specially dyed silks, wools and marked-out designs. In America, Gustav Stickley also sold embroidery kits.

In the 1870s the publishing house of Macmillan and Co. launched their 'Art at Home' series, which included volumes by

William Morris's portrait of Janey Burden as *La Belle Iseult*, painted in 1858. He is said to have written to his future wife, 'I cannot paint you, but I love you'. Tate Gallery, London

Pages from *The Studio*
magazine showing the
winning entries in a
competition to design a
cushion. This was one of
many popular amateur
competitions organized by
the magazine; the majority
of entrants were women

Lucy Faulkner (by then Mrs Orrinsmith),
Walter Crane's sister, Lucy, and the ebul-
lient Mrs Haweis who all gave advice on furnishing and decorating the 'Art' home. The
tone of these books, however, was not to
exhort women merely to take up 'elegant
and useful amusements' but rather to emulate the artists and designers they admired.
'Women have only begun to learn that
there is no market for unskilled labour,'
wrote Mrs M. J. Loftie in Macmillan's *The
Dining-Room*. 'In no employment will ladies
succeed until they cease to be merely amateurs.' More and more women accordingly
enrolled at the new progressive art schools
in Birmingham, Liverpool, Glasgow and
London. At the Arts and Crafts Exhibition
Society exhibitions amateurs, many of them
women, could show their work next to that
of such accomplished designers as Day,
Crane and even Morris himself. *The Studio*
gave serious reviews to these exhibits, especially the textiles, which included everything from *portières* and altar frontals to
book-covers and cot quilts, and often it
illustrated amateur work.

For many women, china-painting or
embroidery did remain just another feminine hobby, but for perhaps thousands it
supplied an escape into active, practical
work, accompanied by the important il-
lusion that they could ally themselves to the
great social and spiritual adventure of the
century and so feel less marginalized by their
own lack of real power over their lives. For
some women, Art work, through the bened-
iction of good taste, allowed them an
entirely respectable and even laudable
means of earning a living. For a very few –
such as Kate Greenaway, Phoebe Traquair,
Hannah Barlow or Jessie M. King – it meant
fame and even fortune.

It was no coincidence that Arts and
Crafts became the style of dress and interior
decoration associated with forward-looking
women. The pioneering Newnham College, Cambridge, for example, a bastion of
women's education, was built by Basil
Champneys in a romantic Queen Anne
revival idiom and furnished and decorated
with Morris and Co. 'Sussex' armchairs and
wallpapers and simple, medieval-style oak
coffers. And Christabel Pankhurst wore a
silver brooch that had been designed by
Ashbee in the form of a stylized flower-
head, set with the suffragette colours – in
amethysts, a cabochon emerald and pearls.

The work of amateur craftspeople,

Contemporary engraving of
Newnham and Girton, the
pioneer women's colleges at
Cambridge. Newnham's
buildings were designed by
Basil Champneys and its
interiors partly furnished by
Morris and Co.

however, highlighted the question that concerned Ashbee after the failure of his Guild: was it enough for people to feel involved in design reform and to enjoy the essential quality of life that he believed accompanied craftsmanship, even if what they produced was without merit or beauty? So many of those who joined Arts and Crafts societies in Europe and America produced work that provoked the belittling description of 'artsy-craftsy'. The question of priorities – aesthetic merit or quality of life – is impossible to resolve: 'Give them their liberty of production and they'll do it better', hoped Ashbee vainly. But the criticism levelled at much of the second-rate amateur work was particularly damaging to the cause of feminism, for poorly conceived or executed designs were seen by some as evidence not of lack of opportunities, training or facilities but of an essential failure in women to meet the challenge of true artistic endeavour.

Agnes Garrett (sister of Elizabeth Garrett Anderson – Kate Greenaway's doctor – and of the feminist Millicent Fawcett) and her cousin Rhoda Garrett found that it took years to discover an architect prepared to take them on and train them as clerks. At last J. M. Brydon, who, in partnership with Bruce Talbert and Daniel Cottier, had run a firm of 'Art Furniture Makers, Glass and Tile Makers', employed them, and eventually they founded their own decorating firm, designing furniture, chimney-pieces and wallpapers in the Queen Anne revival style. They designed furniture (now at Standen) for James Beale's London house in Holland Park. But Rhoda later spoke bitterly of the opposition and prejudice that had faced them. Only in 1907 was a Women's Guild of Arts founded, by May Morris and Mrs Thackeray Turner, wife of a cabinet-maker; it was sponsored by the Art Workers' Guild, which did not itself admit women as members until 1964.

In America, there was not such an ideological force opposed to women making practical use of their skills – skills which had proved essential during the Civil War: the wife of a frontiersman could ill afford to emulate those Society women, described by Edith Wharton, who led 'a temperate life of minor accomplishments . . . child-bearing was their task, needlework their recreation, being respected their privilege'. Many women inspired by the Arts and Crafts movement earned their share of respect not only as artists but as businesswomen, publishers, teachers and innovators.

One of the most influential among American women artists was Candace Wheeler, who had founded Associated Artists with L. C. Tiffany. She was fifty-six years old when her partners left and, with her daughter Dora and her friends Rosina Emmett, Ida Clark and Caroline Townsend, she took over the firm. Not only did they retain such clients as Andrew Carnegie (for whom they created fabric woven with a design of thistles to denote his Scots origin), Cornelius Vanderbilt II and the poet H. W. Longfellow, but they went on to supply designs for wallpapers to the New York manufacturer Warren, Fuller and Co. and for printed and woven textiles to Cheny Brothers of South Manchester, Connecticut. Mrs Wheeler was introduced to Warren, Fuller and Co. after winning a thousand-dollar prize in a design competition they held, but

Portrait plaque by W.S. Coleman at Minton's newly-founded Art-Pottery Studio, Kensington Gore, c.1872

the Cheny and Wheeler families were old friends. The Wheelers were well-travelled, and Dora's designs were much influenced by Walter Crane's style; her mother, on the other hand, strove to introduce specifically American themes into her designs. She especially loved the native flowers and plants, described in the poetry of Ralph Waldo Emerson, and she would sketch them at her remote summer retreat in the Catskill Mountains.

Candace Wheeler wrote many articles and books and also taught at the Cooper Union in New York. Her contribution both to the decorative arts and to the cause of women was recognized when she was appointed Director of Color to the Women's Building at the great World's Columbian Exposition in Chicago in 1893. She was given sole responsibility for the decoration of the library in the Women's Building, which she effected with drapery in shades of blue and green to mirror the water that could be seen through the single, large window. She also had the task of collecting exhibits for the Bureau of Applied Arts, where Associated Artists exhibited a vast 'needlewoven' tapestry faithfully copied

from Raphael's cartoon for the *Miraculous Draught of Fishes.*

Mrs Wheeler had first become involved in a life outside the sphere of her family and friends after the death of her eldest daughter, Daisy, in 1876; at that time she had organized the New York Society of Decorative Art and the Women's Exchange to help women who needed some small independent income: the secretary of the New York Society of Decorative Art was Elizabeth Custer, General Custer's widow, and many war widows were grateful for 'the door to honest effort among women' that Mrs Wheeler had opened.

For many women, the ideals of the Arts and Crafts Movement were easily allied to their traditional concern with philanthropic works. In 1889 in Chicago, Jane Addams founded Hull House, a settlement house modelled on London's Toynbee Hall, where immigrants were taught craft skills. In 1900 a Protestant missionary named Sybil Carter went to work among the Ojibway Indians on the White Earth Reservation in Minnesota. And in 1904, in order to give them some skills whereby they could earn a living, she founded the Indian Lace Association, with the successful idea of teaching the Indians lace-making techniques, though mainly based on Italian rather than local originals. The lace sold well, but did little to preserve the traditional craft skills of the Ojibway Indians. The militant socialist Ellen Gates Starr also found that in order to pay its way at all, a craft workshop had to concentrate on making beautiful objects for the rich. She had left Chicago to study bookbinding in England with T. J. Cobden-Sanderson and returned to set up the Hull House bindery, but disillusioned with what she saw as the failure of the Ruskinian ideal, she eventually retired to a Catholic convent.

In England, too, Art for All, the philanthropic aim of bringing beauty into working-class lives became a vital element of the Arts and Crafts movement, and was often allied to the fervent desire of the middle-classes to revive disappearing rural crafts. Small guilds, such as the Keswick School of Industrial Art, the Yattendon Metalworking Class or the Clarion Guild in Leeds were founded all over the country, often by local ladies, and exhibited their work at the Arts and Crafts Exhibition Society shows. Maude King and Mary Blount, with their husbands, helped to found and run the Haslemere Weaving Industry and the Peasant Art Society, also in Haslemere, with the aim of repopulating and regenerating the countryside: local working-class women produced hand-woven silk, cotton and linen textiles, appliqué embroidery, and hand-woven pile and tapestry carpets.

In 1884 the Home Arts and Industries Association was founded by Mrs Jebb; it was dedicated to the revival of village crafts by amateur craftspeople and inspired by the work of an American, Charles Godfrey Leland, who had established a manual training programme for Philadelphia schools. Within two years, schools or classes had been established in over fifty areas, many of which developed into commercial concerns, and in 1904 *Arts and Crafts* began monthly publication. The Association held regular exhibitions at the Albert Hall in London.

Artistic philanthropy took many forms: Selwyn Image and A. H. Mackmurdo, for example, founded the Fitzroy Picture Society to distribute prints of great paintings to schools; Georgiana Burne-Jones was involved in the establishment of the South London Gallery in Camberwell in 1893, which aimed to exhibit pictures to local poor children without charge; and there were other similar schemes to bring art into tenements and hospitals. Art may not have put bread into hungry mouths or clothed cold, dirty children, but the desire to enfranchise the pleasures of beautiful things did much to alter nineteenth-century attitudes towards the working-class: the 'brutes' and 'dumb animals' of the Chartist risings became the heroes of Morris's socialist Utopia.

'Consider the Lillies of the Field' embroidered and painted *portière*, designed and made by Candace Wheeler in 1879. Mark Twain Memorial, Connecticut

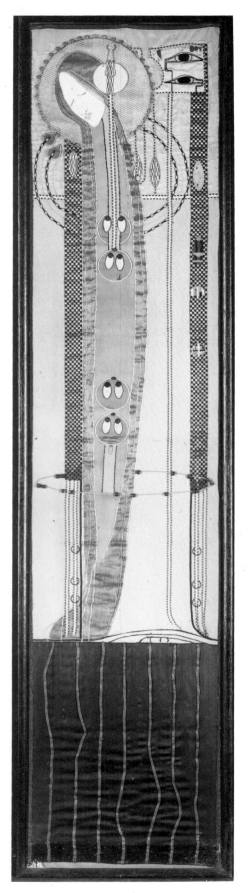

EMBROIDERY

Above left: Embroidered panel designed by May Morris and worked by the Battye family, who commissioned the design; cushion cover (*below left*) designed by Jessie Newbery and embroidered by her mother, Mrs Rowat, *c.*1916; and (*left*) one of a pair of embroidered and appliquéd linen panels, enhanced with glass beads, metal thread, braid and ribbon, designed by Margaret Macdonald Mackintosh and exhibited in the 'Rose Boudoir' at the Turin International Exhibition in 1902

Janey Morris, the medieval chatelaine of Morris's Red House, was taught by her husband how to do simple woollen crewel work, and she became an accomplished embroideress. Her sister, Elizabeth Burden, became chief instructress at the Royal School of Art Needlework, opened in South Kensington in 1872. The women associated with the School were not, however, encouraged to design their own work, but only to execute designs by Morris, Burne-Jones, Crane and others.

May Morris, who took over the Morris and Co. embroidery section in 1885, produced well-spaced, light, floral designs for curtains, table-cloths, cushion covers, cot quilts and work-bags, as well as executing work designed by her father. In 1893 she published *Decorative Needlework*, and in 1910 undertook a lecture tour of America.

Gertrude Jekyll, inspired by a meeting with Morris in the 1860s also became a talented needlewoman and won commissions from Lord Leighton and the Duke of Westminster. She was forced by failing eyesight to abandon close work and concentrate on garden design.

Jessie Newbery, wife of the principal of Glasgow School of Art, established embroidery classes there in 1894. Many of her students intended to become primary- and secondary-school teachers, and Mrs Newbery rejected the highly skilled intricacy of the Royal School of Art Needlework, favouring instead simpler techniques, such as appliqué, and cheaper materials that could be used in local schools. 'I specially aim at beautifully shaped spaces,' she wrote, 'and try to make them as important as the patterns.' It was her assistant, Ann Macbeth, who, in *Educational Needlecraft*,

the book she wrote in 1911 with Margaret Swanson, publicized Jessie Newbery's approach, as well as suggesting new ways of teaching primary-school children to sew and encouraging them to use embroidery as a means of self-expression.

Jessie Newbery's influence can be seen in the work of Frances and Margaret Macdonald, who were students at the School of Art and who opened their studio in Glasgow in 1896, producing not only embroidery but also gesso, book illustrations and metalwork. After her marriage to Charles Rennie Mackintosh in 1900, Margaret used embroidery within schemes he designed for interior decoration at the Turin International Exhibition of 1902, and in the Willow Tea-Rooms and Hill House near Glasgow. Her elongated female figures were strikingly realized through stylized appliqué with added beads, ribbon, braid and metal threads.

In England, there was a resurgence of interest in many traditional rural techniques, such as smocking: in America, too, needlework skills such as quilting were revived. In 1896 Margaret Whiting and Ellen Miller founded the Society of Blue and White Needlework in Deerfield, Massachusetts. Initially they adapted old designs, worked in blue thread on a white ground, but then began to create their own designs, using multi-coloured threads and appliqué on coloured fabric. They exhibited their work at Arts and Crafts Society exhibitions in Boston, New York and Chicago. At the H. Sophie Newcomb College for Women in New Orleans, students used the colours and forms of local flora and fauna in their embroidery designs.

AMERICAN CERAMICS

In Cincinnati, Maria Longworth Nichols turned her hobby of china-painting into a highly successful business – the Rookwood Pottery – when, in 1880, she persuaded her wealthy father to turn an old schoolhouse on the Ohio River into a pottery. The work of the pottery was divided, with different people in charge of throwing, firing and decorating. Laura A. Fry developed the atomizing technique that was used to spray a smooth coloured glaze on to the surface of Rookwood's 'Standard' ware; Matthew A. Daly was responsible for the striking portraits of 'Native Americans'; and many other decorators painted the countless flowers and landscapes that made up the various lines, known as 'Sea Green', 'Iris', 'Aerial Blue', and a series with matt glazes, the most successful of which was 'Vellum'. In 1886 Maria Nichols remarried and thereafter became less involved in the running of Rookwood, which dominated the American pottery market until it closed in 1941.

Louise McLaughlin, also from Cincinnati, returned from the Philadelphia Centennial Exposition inspired by the slip-painted stoneware produced for Limoges by Ernest Chaplet. Already an accomplished china-painter, she now began experimenting herself and in 1878 produced her own 'Cincinnati Limoges'. Ten years later, she went on to experiment with porcelain clays in a kiln in her back yard and in 1898 produced her 'Losanti' ware.

Adelaide Alsop Robineau taught herself china decoration from books, and went on to teach it and, in 1899, to edit *Keramic Studio* magazine, which contained designs and information for china-painters. Longing for more control over the form of her work, she began experimenting with throwing and firing and in 1903 turned to porcelain, fired at extremely high temperatures to achieve distinctive crystalline glaze effects. She also used the time-consuming decorative technique of incising into the clay body. Within two years her work was on sale at Tiffany and Co. in New York. She was involved with the short-lived University City Pottery in Missouri, where she created her prize-winning 'Scarab Vase', which took one thousand hours to complete.

Standard glaze pottery portrait vase of a North American Indian chief decorated by Grace Young at the Rookwood Pottery, Cincinnati, Ohio in 1905; 'Foxes and Grapes' high-glazed earthenware vase (*opposite left*), with incised decoration, made by Adelaide Robineau in Syracuse in 1922; and (*right*) a ceramic pot decorated by Leona Nicholson and fired at Newcomb College, New Orleans, 1910-15

In 1895 a pottery was established at the H. Sophie Newcomb College in New Orleans, where students were encouraged to explore their own visual ideas. They created a distinctive style, using simple, incised decoration combined with bold, bright colours to portray local plants, trees and animals: magnolia, poinsettia, rice, cotton, Cherokee rose or cypress trees appeared in confident, spontaneous forms.

FASHION

Dress reform, especially the lobby against the unhealthy practice of tight-lacing, had been gathering momentum since the 1840s. The American Free Dress League was founded in 1874, and 'reform' garments were displayed at the 1876 Philadelphia Centennial Exposition. In London, Mrs King founded the Rational Dress Society in 1881; its *Gazette* championed the abolition of the corset and the adoption of the divided skirt.

From Janey Morris and Georgiana Burne-Jones onwards, many of the women associated with the Arts and Crafts movement wore loose, uncorseted 'reform' clothes, and Burne-Jones objected when in the 1880s his wife took the reactionary step of wearing a bustle. C. R. Ashbee's wife Janet, who attended meetings of the Healthy and Artistic Dress Union, removed her stays on her honeymoon and never wore them again. She also wore sandals with bare feet, even in London.

Several painters and architects turned their attention to women's fashion and designed loose, flowing 'Art' clothes. E. W. Godwin became director of Liberty's costume department in 1884; Henri van de Velde's 'reform' clothes were unveiled at Krefeld, the centre of the German textile industry, in 1900; Frank Lloyd Wright designed dresses for his wife, Catherine, and even for clients; and, in Vienna, Gustav Klimt designed the wondrous, embroidered dresses that appeared in his paintings, and were made by his lover, Emilie Flöge. The fashion atelier set up at the Wiener Werkstätte in 1910 was directed by Edouard Wimmer, and produced everything from beaded evening bags to pyjamas, evening cloaks to millinery. Couturiers such as Fortuny in Italy or Natalia Lamanova in Moscow all helped to create this new image of women.

In *The Art of Beauty*, Mrs Haweis recommended the ideal background for the modern woman, with oak furniture and dark tapestries in rooms where harmony would replace brilliance and detail would become important; women, she advised, should abandon loud patterns and gaudy colours for loosely draped clothes in soft colours,

worn with delicate jewellery. In the 1870s, various books of this sort paid homage to the influence of such contemporary icons as Janey Morris and the other Pre-Raphaelite models. These images had imbued female beauty with an ethereal spirituality and made it something to be worshipped. They contributed towards the cult of women that flourished in a variety of images, ranging from the medieval damozel, the golden goddesses of Alma-Tadema's paintings or the simpering angels of the portrait plaques painted by W. S. Coleman for Minton's, to the morbid sexuality of the Medusa and Salomé figures of the French Symbolists. Actresses such as Ellen Terry, Lillie Langtry, Eleonora Duse and Sarah Bernhardt were important role-models: Bernhardt, particularly, inspired the jewellery of René Lalique and Georges Fouquet and the posters of Alphonse Mucha.

Three influential women: Janey Morris in 1865 (*opposite*), posed for her photograph by Dante Gabriel Rossetti, who painted her often (Victoria & Albert Museum, London); the Viennese couturier Emilie Flöge (*right*) painted in 1902 by Gustav Klimt who designed dresses made by Emilie and her sister; and (*overleaf*) a poster by Alphonse Mucha of Sarah Bernhardt as *La Dame aux Camelias*. Historisches Museum der Stadt, Vienna

JEWELLERY

Top: Tinted horn tiara set with moonstones in the form of elderberries, made by Fred Partridge and retailed by Liberty and Co., *c.*1900; (*left*) a breast ornament of gold, set with moonstones, rubies, chrysoprase and abalone shell, designed by John Paul Cooper in 1908 and (*right*) a corsage ornament in silver and gold, set with garnets and pearls, probably designed by C.R. Ashbee for the Guild of Handicraft

Previous page: Brooch and two belt buckles of enamelled silver by Nelson and Edith B. Dawson

Arts and Crafts jewellery, with its use of enamel, semi-precious stones, baroque pearls and inexpensive materials such as horn, provided an alternative to the flashy South African diamonds and sentimental butterflies and flowers, or sporting motifs, beloved by many Victorians. Pugin and Burges both designed Gothic pieces – in gold decorated in bright enamels with such emblems as fleurs-de-lys, roses or doves – and the 'archaeological' jewellery of Carlo Guiliano and Alessandro Castellani was popular among both the Pre-Raphaelites and the aristocratic and artistic group known as The Souls. The Aesthetes also adopted antique jewels, long strings of amber or jade beads, Japanese-style *cloisonné* enamels or the Indian jewellery sold by Liberty's.

But it was Ashbee who totally broke the mould, creating unpretentious, versatile necklaces, pendants, brooches and clasps, often of light silver or gold chain linking his favourite semi-precious materials – moonstones, opals, garnets, amethysts, turquoises and pearls. In later years he also used a shimmering turquoise enamel. His naturalistic forms of flowers, birds and butterflies, although simple, were richly expressive of his ideals.

Ashbee's style was echoed in the work both of Nelson Dawson, who had studied enamelling under Alexander Fisher, and of his wife Edith, a watercolourist. The same influence was evident too in the intricate but delicate and unassuming pieces made in Birmingham by the illustrator Georgina Gaskin and her husband, the wood-engraver Arthur Gaskin, who in 1902 became the head of the Vittoria Street School for Jewellers and Silversmiths.

The Gaskins were among the many artists supplying Liberty's. Fred Partridge, who had been a member of Ashbee's Guild, continued with his wife May Hart to produce carved pieces in coloured horn at their Soho workshop. His work – for example, a tiara in the form of elderberries in purple-tinted horn decorated with moonstones – was perhaps influenced by that of René Lalique. Ella Napper, who worked with Partridge, also supplied Liberty's, as did Murrle Bennett and Co., Arthur Silver, Archibald Knox and Jessie M. King.

The apparent simplicity of much Arts and Crafts jewellery gave way to more sumptuous work, such as the amazing enamelled gold creations of Henry Wilson, which were studded with bizarre jewels, including baroque pearls, opals, rock crystals, star sapphires and mother-of-pearl. John Paul Cooper and Edward Spencer, who designed metalwork and jewellery, were both influenced by his style.

In America, many jewellers and metalworkers were women; for example, Florence Koehler in Chicago, Madeleine Yale Wynne in Deerfield, Massachusetts, and Elizabeth Copeland in Boston. In 1900 Clara Barck, a graduate of the Art Institute of Chicago, founded the Kalo Shops as an all-women workshop producing weaving and leather-goods. The name was derived from the Greek word *kalos*, meaning 'beautiful', and their motto was 'Beautiful, Useful, and Enduring'. In 1905, after her marriage to an amateur metalworker, George Welles, Clara Barck established the Kalo Art-Crafts Community as both a workshop and a school, and began to create simple and elegant jewellery and tablewares with the hammered surface texture inspired by Ashbee.

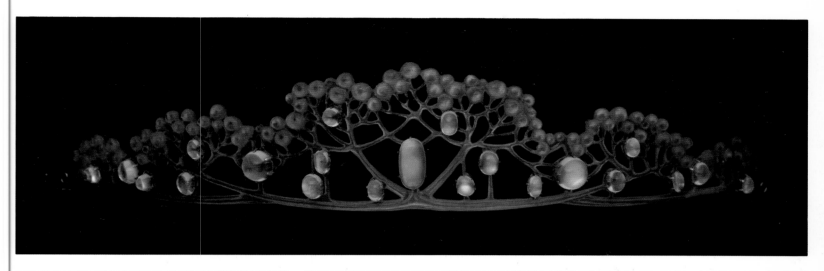

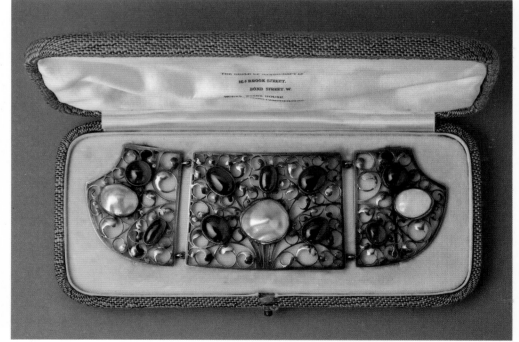

Part Four

INTO THE TWENTIETH CENTURY

New Departures

The widespread economic expansion of the 1890s led to a demand for houses, villas and apartment blocks from a new type of client. The European industrialists and financiers who looked forward with such confidence to the new century wanted houses and furnishings that were modern and which reflected the forward-looking outlook that had won them their wealth. In England, the newly-rich patronized Arts and Crafts architects, but the English love of rural traditions led ultimately to the Home Counties style later dubbed 'Stockbroker Tudor'. In Berlin, Vienna and Paris, however, new money wanted an entirely new style.

For the artists and architects of the European Secession movements, the desire to free art and design from sterile historicism was a vital part of their creed. While the English became increasingly concerned with the preservation of rural traditions, in Europe those inspired by the writings of Morris and Ruskin and the designs of Ashbee, Mackmurdo or Crane, developed their own visual imageries. The sinuous curves and tendrils of Art Nouveau – a 'new art' inspired by natural forms – appeared in France in the work of Louis Majorelle, Eugène Grasset, Georges de Feure, Edward Colonna and Eugène Gaillard; in Holland

in the work of the architect Hendrik Berlage and the artist Jan Toorop; and in Belgium in the wrought iron and mosaics of Victor Horta's Maison Tassel and Hôtel Solvay, the town houses of Paul Hankar and the furniture of Gustave Serrurier-Bovy.

One of the most influential figures of this new style was the Belgian painter Henri van de Velde. He was a member of the Société des Vingt, founded in 1884 to promote the work of avant-garde painters, including many of the French Post-Impressionists. Influenced by the Arts and Crafts Exhibition Society show held in Brussels in 1891, van de Velde turned to the decorative arts, and went on to design furniture, interiors, silver, ceramics, textiles, books and typography. In 1896 the four interiors he contributed to Samuel Bing's Maison de l'Art Nouveau in Paris brought him to the attention of French designers, and by the turn of the century he had settled in Berlin. In 1902 he was appointed artistic adviser on arts and industries to the Grand Duke of Saxe-Weimar, and he founded the Weimar Kunstgewerbeschule, which later became the Staatliches Bauhaus. In 1914, as a founder member of the Deutsche Werkbund, he was still adding to the debate on the role of the artist in designing for mass production,

Staircase in the Hotel van Ettvelde, a private mansion in Brussels, designed by Victor Horta in 1897–9

Detail of a carved glass vase by Emile Gallé, 1890s

which, in the decade before war, became the great argument among architects and designers inspired by the Arts and Crafts movement.

In Italy, too, the 'awakening' of the decorative arts in *Stile Floreale* and *Stile Liberty* coincided with the increasing industrialization of the country and so heightened awareness among designers of the need to co-operate with manufacturers and industrialists. Nevertheless, at the International Exhibition held in Turin in 1902, although no reproductions of past styles were allowed, the principal buildings, by Raimonda d'Aronco, were in an ornate Byzantine style, which was echoed in the Moorish tassels and arches of Carlo Bugatti's 'Thousand and One Nights' furniture. It was at Turin that Bugatti unveiled his extraordinary 'Snail Room' – one of four interiors containing almost sculptural furniture decorated with painted vellum, intricate inlaid metals and carved wood; Bugatti also produced sculptural pieces of silverware and jewellery. However, in 1904 he left Milan for Paris, though his furniture continued to be made under licence by the Milan firm of De Vecchi.

The Milanese cabinet-maker Eugenio Quarti, a friend of Bugatti's (who also made luxurious furniture, carved and inlaid with mother-of-pearl and metal), put some elegant pieces, painted white and decorated with stencilled flowers, into the Turin Exhibition. By the time of the Milan International Exposition four years later, however, Pietro Zen, son of the Art Nouveau furniture designer Carlo Zen, was showing furniture designed for industrial production.

In Europe, there was less concern about what would now be termed the 'lifestyle' of the craftsman, and few were concerned with establishing guilds that specifically protected the craftsman's way of life according to medieval ideals. The aspect of Morris's writings that most concerned the Europeans was the vital importance of one's daily environment, and the belief that its simplicity, restraint and fitness for purpose in the home, office or street could influence people for the good. The means by which the economic expansion of the 1890s had been achieved – better communications, faster forms of travel, more powerful industrial machinery, greater numbers of workers employed in factories and offices – had made European cities even busier, more crowded, noisy and dirty. The plain interiors offered by the Arts and Crafts movement, full of calm and integrity, presented a haven of peace and clear thinking.

The luxury of Art Nouveau or *Stile Floreale* was gradually rejected in favour of a new, sophisticated idiom which took as its starting point 'truth to nature' – a truth variously interpreted in the 1860s by Ruskin or Dresser, but which was now reduced to a spatial geometry. This not only provided visual calm and ease, but also had the advantage – for the social aims of the Arts and Crafts movement were still present – that designs based on such a geometry could be made cheaply and in great numbers by machine, and so be available not just to the wealthy who could afford hand-craftsmanship, but to ordinary working people. For many, it was an exciting ideal, but for those who shared Morris's hatred of industrialization, it was anathema.

One of the first architects to move, not in

Opposite: Chair by Carlo Bugatti in wood overlaid with painted parchment, and with inlaid copper; one of a set of four exhibited in his *Salle de Jeu et de Conversation* at the Turin Exposition of 1902. Virginia Museum of Fine Arts

The hall in Hill House, Helensburgh, designed by C.R. Mackintosh

the direction of mass production, but towards a geometric harmony of building and interior, was the Scotsman Charles Rennie Mackintosh. Although the English hated his early work, especially his exaggerated, stylized graphics, he was enormously influential in Europe, where his work was seen in the late 1890s in *The Studio* and in *Deutsche Kunst und Dekoration* and *Dekorative Kunst*, and he had several followers in Glasgow. E. A. Taylor, a former shipyard draughtsman, came under the influence of the 'Glasgow Four' – Mackintosh, his wife Margaret Macdonald, her sister Frances and her husband Herbert MacNair – at the School of Art; John Ednie and George Logan, whose work was influenced equally by Mackintosh and by Baillie Scott, both designed complete interiors for the large Glasgow firm of Wylie and Lockhead in a watered-down form of the Glasgow style; and George Walton, who worked as a decorator on several houses in the Glasgow area before moving to London (where he designed furniture, fitments and shopfronts for the Kodak Company), also borrowed elements of Mackintosh's style.

In the summer of 1900, a wealthy Viennese banker, Fritz Wärndorfer, visited Glasgow, admired the work of the 'Glasgow Four' and invited them to exhibit with the eighth Secessionist exhibition.

Charles and Margaret Mackintosh visited Vienna, where they showed some of the furniture from their Mains Street flat, together with two gesso panels from Mackintosh's Ingram Street tea-rooms and some other items. They met many of the founding members of the Secession, including Josef Hoffmann, and must have been struck by the lively intellectual climate of the Viennese coffee-houses, for this was the Vienna of Freud, Wittgenstein, Mahler, Schönberg, and Musil, where every branch of philosophy, literature and the arts was under examination.

Mackintosh and Hoffmann met again at the Turin Exhibition in 1902, for which Mackintosh had designed the Scottish pavilion. He and Margaret contributed a white, silver and pink 'Rose Boudoir', based on three gesso panels by Margaret, together with Mackintosh's elegant black and white furniture. Frances and Herbert MacNair (who had left Glasgow for Liverpool, where MacNair now taught) designed a writing room, and two further rooms contained work by Jessie M. King, her future husband E. A. Taylor and George Logan. Meeting again in Turin with the banker Wärndorfer, Charles and Margaret were commissioned by him to design a music salon for his house in Vienna. Later that year Wärndorfer and Hoffmann visited Glasgow to discuss their plans for a decorative arts workshop with the couple.

The Wiener Werkstätte, with an architectural office and workshops producing metalwork, bookbinding and leatherwork, wood- and lacquerwork, was established in premises in Neustiftgasse in October 1903; the enterprise was financed by Wärndorfer,

and Hoffmann and Koloman Moser were artistic directors. They considered themselves responsible for every element of an interior, from cutlery to light fittings, and even designed individual keys. As a result of their rigorous rejection of shoddy mass production and the 'mindless imitation of old styles', everything for the new premises, including their distinctive graphics and lettering, was designed afresh by Hoffmann and Moser. In this they were wholeheartedly supported by Mackintosh, who wrote in a letter to Hoffmann: '. . . every object which you release must be most definitely marked by individuality, beauty and the utmost accuracy of execution. Your aim must above all be that every object you produce should have been made for a particular purpose and place.'

Hoffmann also insisted on the best working conditions for his craftsmen. In their 'Working Programme' of 1905, Moser and Hoffmann wrote: 'We neither can nor will compete for the lowest prices – that is chiefly done at the worker's expense. We, on the contrary, regard it as our highest duty to return him to a position in which he can take pleasure in his labour and lead a life in keeping with human dignity.'

The style of the early years of the Wiener Werkstätte was largely non-representational, relying on colourless, geometric grids offset by the opulent silverware designed by Hoffmann or Carl Otto Czeschka, the smart black and white ceramics produced by Bertold Löffler and Michael Powolny at the Wiener Keramik, and the cabinets designed by Moser with elaborate veneers and inlays. In their contrast between a spare, geometric formality and touches of luxury, the Wiener Werkstätte interiors were similar in conception to the collaboration between Mackintosh, with his often stark furniture, and his wife, who contributed rich, figurative gesso or embroidered panels to his early interiors. But while Mackintosh moved towards greater coherence and apparent simplicity, the Wiener Werkstätte thrived on sales of its more frivolous luxury goods.

Their most exotic commission was for the Palais Stoclet, a mansion built in Brussels for the great Belgian collector and railway 'king', Adolphe Stoclet, and described by his granddaughter as 'a house for angels'. Begun in 1905, it took eight years of planning and construction, and almost bankrupted the workshops. Precious materials such as polychrome marbles, malachite, onyx and bronze were used throughout: the mosaic friezes, *Expectation* and *Fulfilment*, designed by Gustav Klimt for the dining-room, contained coral, semi-precious stones and gold.

Yet despite the increasing success of the Wiener Werkstätte's jewellery, lace, bead bags, toys, postcards (some designed by Oskar Kokoschka) or Christmas decorations, Hoffmann's concern for the improved organization of the workshops continued. In 1909 the Vienna Kunstgewerbeschule had been reformed according to Arts and Crafts principles, with greater emphasis on practical workshop experience. In 1913 Hoffmann extended this practice and established the Kunstlerwerkstätte, where artists, many of whom were Hoffmann's former students from the Kunstgewerbeschule, could come and experiment with a wide range of media under

Left: Painted terracotta head by Gudrun Baudisch for the Wiener Werkstätte, c.1927

the guidance of experienced master-craftsmen. This saved young artists the expense of setting up their own workshops, and the Wiener Werkstätte, who reserved the right to buy any of the designs produced in the Kunstlerwerkstätte, was provided with a steady source of fresh ideas.

After the decimation of the First World War, followed by the influenza epidemic of 1918 in which Otto Wagner, Kolo Moser, Gustav Klimt and Egon Schiele all died, the Kunstlerwerkstätte was dominated by women. Mathilde Flögl, who became Hoffmann's chief collaborator, Maria Likarz, Fritzi Löw and Hilda Jesser designed wallpapers and textiles for the Wiener Werkstätte, while a new generation of potters – Vally Wieselthier, Susie Singer and Gudrun

Opposite: Photograph of Margaret Macdonald Mackintosh in 1900, sitting beside a cabinet designed by her husband

Baudisch – produced boldly coloured, expressionistic, figurative ceramics.

In Germany, encouraged by the powerful figure of Hermann Muthesius, the guilds, or Werkstätten, were encouraged to find commercial success not through luxury goods but through mass production. In 1905 Bruno Paul at the Munich Vereinigte Werkstätten had begun experimenting with 'Typenmöbel', unit furniture which used laminated timber sheets and standardized components, but the success of the workshops – by 1907 they employed six hundred workers and had branch offices in Hamburg, Bremen and Berlin – still depended on the huge variety of products they offered which, although often made using machines, were not mass produced. In Dresden, Richard Riemerschmid was studying the feasibility of 'Maschinenmöbel'. Peter Behrens, who had become dissatisfied with the artists' colony in Darmstadt, had been appointed by Muthesius as director of the Düsseldorf School of Applied Arts in 1903. He became a leading spokesman for the idea of *Typesierung*, standardization for mass production. In 1906 he began his association with AEG, the Allgemeine Elektrizitäts Gesellschaft (General Electric Company) in Berlin, where he was to persuade the company to furnish their workers' houses with 'Typenmöbel'.

Ideas about mass production were very much in the air when the Deutsche Werkbund was founded in 1907. The Werkbund, the brainchild of Muthesius, was an association of individual craftsmen, designers, architects and workshops – including the Werkstätten in Munich, Dresden and elsewhere – and other commercial and industrial concerns. The Werkbund's aim was to put an end to poor quality mass-produced goods by encouraging the creation of individually-designed objects through exhibitions, lectures and other forms of publicity. Behrens, Riemerschmid and van de Velde in Germany and Olbrich and the Wiener Werkstätte from Vienna were among the founding members.

There was no coherent Werkbund style, as the Werkbund *Yearbook*s show: illustrations of aeroplanes or railway stations appear next to hand-crafted objects. But its influence grew steadily, especially through the art schools (Behrens was in Düsseldorf, Riemerschmid in Munich and Bruno Paul in Berlin) and it attracted many new members. At the Werkbund exhibition held in Cologne in 1914, there was work by van de Velde and, in the Austrian pavilion, designed by Hoffmann in classical style, the essentially decorative artist, Dagobert Peche, had a room to himself; yet there was also work by Behrens, Bruno Taut and Walter Gropius, who exhibited a prototype factory with a glass façade revealing the machinery inside. At the exhibition, however, van de Velde, supported by Walter Gropius, clashed with Muthesius on the sore issue of artistic individuality versus total standardization. Although van de Velde welcomed modern materials and machine production, he declared that: 'The artist is essentially and intimately a passionate individualist, a spontaneous creator. Never will he, of his own free will, submit to a discipline forcing upon him a norm, a canon.' The argument raged on in one form or another throughout the 1920s and 1930s, and has yet to be resolved.

Stained and painted wood dresser designed by Peter Behrens for the Deutsche Werkbund, c.1902

CHARLES RENNIE MACKINTOSH

Leaded glass panel by the Scottish designer George Walton, after a
design of stylized roses by C.R. Mackintosh

Charles Rennie Mackintosh (1868–1928), the son of a superintendent of police, trained as an architect in Glasgow in the offices of Honeyman and Keppie, where he met Herbert MacNair. Together they attended evening classes at the Glasgow School of Art, which had recently been reorganized on Arts and Crafts principles by its new head, Francis Newbery. There they met Margaret and Frances Macdonald, and the 'Glasgow Four', as they became known, began to collaborate on decorative schemes.

They exhibited posters and metalwork at the Arts and Crafts Exhibition Society in London in 1896, but their work was heavily criticized for being distorted and unnatural. The new Scottish style was dubbed the 'Spook School'; nevertheless, they found a champion in Gleeson White, editor of *The Studio*, who visited Glasgow and wrote admiringly of their work.

In 1897 Mackintosh won the competition to design the new Glasgow School of Art, which was completed in 1909. The overall scheme had an integrity and vitality which marked a radical departure from existing vernacular styles, using metalwork especially to reinforce the thematic elements. Mackintosh frequently echoed the massive outlines and vivid history of Scottish castles in his own buildings, combining a protective monumentality, enhanced by energized ornamental details, with an imaginative conception of interior space.

In 1899 he began to collaborate with Margaret Macdonald, whom he married the following year. Their flat at 120 Mains Street, Glasgow, demonstrated his concerns for interior decoration. No pattern was allowed except occasional stylized motifs embroidered by Margaret or contained in leaded-glass or metalwork panels inset into his furniture – though Mackintosh's distinctive arrangements of woven twigs formed one other permitted element. The colour scheme was in grey, black and white, and the harmony of the room lay in its proportions. Some of the furniture from the flat was shown in 1900 at the eighth Secession Exhibition in Vienna, where the couple's work was warmly received by Josef Hoffmann and other members of the Secession.

During the next few years, Mackintosh received several major commissions: for Miss Cranston's tea-rooms in Ingram Street and Willow Street, Glasgow, for Miss Cranston's own house, Hous'hill (also in Glasgow), and for two other private houses – Windyridge at Kilmacolm, and Hill House, Helensburgh, for the publisher William Blackie. In these two houses, he began to curtail his use of Margaret's stylized images, whether in gesso panels or embroidery, and to rely entirely on proportion and geometry for his effects.

In 1904 he became a partner in Honeyman and Keppie, but little new work came his way, and in 1913 he resigned from the firm. Cut off from his friends in Vienna by the war, he left Glasgow and in 1915 settled in Chelsea, where he received a few minor architectural commissions and he and Margaret designed some abstract and stylized textiles. In 1920 the couple moved to the south of France, where he painted watercolours. He died of cancer in London in 1928.

Top: Charles Rennie Mackintosh

Above: Watercolour study of polyanthus flowers, painted by C.R.
Mackintosh in 1915

Right: The main bedroom at Hill House, Helensburgh, by C.R.
Mackintosh

JOSEF HOFFMANN AND THE WIENER WERKSTÄTTE

Josef Hoffmann (1870–1956) studied architecture in Munich and in Otto Wagner's office in Vienna, where he met J. M. Olbrich. In 1897 he joined the Secession, where, with Koloman Moser, an illustrator who had studied at the Vienna Kunstgewerbeschule, he was responsible for exhibiting decorative arts – especially those by British Arts and Crafts movement designers. When the Secessionist painter Felician von Myerbach became principal of the Kunstgewerbeschule in 1899, Hoffmann and Moser were appointed to the staff. Hoffmann's influence on generations of students was immense.

Both Hoffmann and Moser considered Biedermeier to have been the last true 'style', and they argued for greater simplicity and restraint in the design of furniture and everyday objects. In 1903, after a visit by Hoffmann and the banker Fritz Wärndorfer to England, the Wiener Werkstätte (the Vienna Workshop) was established, inspired by the example of Ashbee's Guild of Handicraft and by the work of the 'Glasgow Four'.

Hoffmann's architectural commissions – such as a sanatorium at Puckersdorf, near Vienna, the black-and-white-tiled Cabarett Fledermaus in Vienna's Kärntnerstrasse, and the Palais Stoclet in Brussels – were now handled by the Wiener Werkstätte, for whom he designed furniture, jewellery, glass, metalwork and textiles until 1931.

By 1905 the Wiener Werkstätte employed one hundred craftworkers to execute designs by thirty-seven masters and could produce everything for the complete artistic interior. The workshops even offered garden designs, undertaken by Hoffmann's pupil, Franz Lebisch. There were separate departments for metalwork, ceramics, glass, enamelwork, leatherwork, bookbinding, graphics (they produced postcards, posters and theatre programmes), wallpapers, textiles and furniture. The luxury goods, especially the gold tablewares and jewellery or millinery, hand-printed textiles and bead bags, were the height of fashion, and clients included leading actresses, couturiers and artists.

Wiener Werkstätte postcard of the Cabarett Fledermaus, decorated by the workshops in 1907

Moser, tired of dealing with difficult clients, resigned as artistic director in 1907 after financial troubles, and devoted himself to painting and stage design.

In 1914 the workshops were reorganized when Wärndorfer withdrew and left for America. The industrialist Otto Primavesi then took over as financial backer, and outlets were opened in Zurich, Marienbad, Breslau and, briefly, in New York. In the 1920s the Wiener Werkstätte reflected the mood of the post-war years, and the various workshops' style came to be dominated by the more exotic and piquant work of designers such as Carl Otto Czeschka, Vally Wieselthier, Edouard Wimmer, the head of the fashion department which had been set up 1910, and Dagobert Peche, who introduced 'spiky Baroque' – a style inspired by folk-art, and using flowers, animals and human figures as decorative motifs.

In 1928 the Wiener Werkstätte celebrated its twenty-fifth anniversary, but in 1927 there had been political riots in Vienna, and in 1929 the ceramic workshop had to be closed down following the Wall Street Crash. The workshops went into final liquidation in 1931.

Above: Electroplated silver basket designed by Josef Hoffmann, *c.* 1905

Right: Gold cigarette case set with opals, lapis, turquoises, mother-of-pearl, agate and semi-precious stones, designed by Josef Hoffmann for the Wiener Werkstätte in 1912

RICHARD RIEMERSCHMID

Richard Riemerschmid (1868–1957) trained as a painter in Munich. His first designs for furniture, in a neo-Gothic style, were produced in 1895 when he married the actress Ida Hofmann and was furnishing their new apartment. In 1897, when the Vereinigte Werkstätten were established, he started designing metalwork, in wrought iron and bronze, copper and brass, in an unadorned yet sinuous form of Art Nouveau. He also began to contribute designs to both the Vereinigte Werkstätten and other commercial firms for porcelain, glass, cutlery, lighting fixtures, carpets and, from 1905, furnishing textiles with small geometric motifs. His designs were elegant and coherent, with a powerful abstract, sculptural sense of form. His simple, often daring designs, such as the chair exhibited in his 'Music Room' in Dresden in 1899, led the way within the 'functionalist' wing of the Munich *Jugendstil* movement.

Riemerschmid also worked with the Vereinigte Werkstätten für Kunst in Handwerk founded in Dresden by his brother-in-law Karl Schmidt in 1898. In 1906 he designed his 'Maschinenmöbel', reasonably priced suites of machine-made furniture inspired by 'the spirit of the machine', for the Dresdener Werkstätten. The following year the workshops began to concentrate on serial, or mass, production, and Riemerschmid himself became a founding member of the Deutsche Werkbund.

Also in 1907 the Dresden and Munich Werkstätten amalgamated, and together worked on plans for Germany's first garden city at Hellerau near Dresden. Apart from houses, the plans included laundries, a theatre, a training school and the Werkstätten's own workshops. Le Corbusier, who was working in Peter Behrens's office, spent some time at Hellerau, and the arguments he later put forward in *L'Esprit nouveau* have much in common with Riemerschmid's ideas. Riemerschmid believed that design must grow out of modern life, and that it was artefacts such as liners, locomotives or machinery that were truly expressive of the age. 'Life, not art, creates style. It is not made, it grows.'

In 1913 he was appointed director of the Munich Kunstgewerbeschule, where he remained until 1924.

Above: Wine glasses from the 'Menzel' service designed by Richard Riemerschmid in 1903 and made by Benedikt von Poschinger, Oberzwieselau, using a revival of an old glass-making technique

Opposite left: Oak chair designed by Richard Riemerschmid and made by the Vereinigte Werkstätten für Kunst in Handwerk, Munich; exhibited in the Music Room at the Dresden Deutsche Kunst-Ausstellung in 1899

Opposite right: One of a pair of gilt cast brass candlesticks designed by Richard Riemerschmid and made by the Vereinigte Werkstätten für Kunst in Handwerk, Munich in 1897

TEXTILES

The 1890s were a period of great sophistication in textile design, and British fabrics were sold all over world, influencing designers in Europe and America. William Morris championed the use of natural dyes, flat patterning and romantic English flowers. Interest in the 'old English garden', as well as the popular botany taught by Dr Christopher Dresser, greatly influenced textile design. G. P. Baker, for example, of the Kent textile firm G. P. and J. Baker, collected alpine plants and experimented with hybrid irises, and designers such as Lindsay P. Butterfield, George C. Haité and C. F. A. Voysey all used naturalistic flowers in their pattern designs, as did Candace Wheeler in America.

Morris had also studied historical textiles, including medieval French, Italian, English and also Persian examples. His associate Thomas Wardle was interested in Indian chintzes, while the Baker brothers, who had been brought up in Turkey, based their early designs on Isnik patterns.

Although Morris and Co. produced ornate tapestry and embroidered hangings, the greatest demand was for the printed furnishing cottons known as cretonnes. Washable patterned cottons were especially popular in smoky cities for curtains (often with matching window-seat cushions) and for upholstery. Warner and Sons, a former Spitalfields silk-weaving firm which moved to Essex in 1895, produced conventionalized designs by Owen Jones, Japanese-inspired designs by Bruce Talbert and the flowing, proto-Art Nouveau patterns by A. H. Mackmurdo; the Lancashire firm of Turnbull and Stockdale, where Lewis F. Day was artistic director from 1881, was another major supplier of furnishing fabrics.

In Europe, it became common for architects and artists to design textiles. However, the Art Nouveau stylization of Henri van de Velde or Alphonse Mucha, and the geometric patterning of Richard Riemerschmid or Josef Hoffmann gave way to abstract patterning, and by 1914 the heyday of the 'artist-designed' textile was over.

Top: 'King Cup', ink and watercolour design for a printed linen by Jessie M. King, *c.*1925. Printed by Thomas Wardle for Liberty and Co.
Above: Lace panel designed for the Wiener Werkstätte by Dagobert Peche
Opposite: Woven silk, wool and cotton double cloth designed by Lindsay P. Butterfield for Alexander Morton and Co. in 1898

A Second Generation
Interprets the Style

The first years of the new century saw the development of a harmonious form of ornament based on natural geometry, an 'organic' form of design which could be reflected in all aspects of a house, from its relationship to the surrounding landscape to its furnishings and decorative motifs. The importance of using local materials and of binding a house to its landscape resulted in the emergence of distinctive regional styles of architecture and design.

The most famous of all such styles was that of the Prairie School, developed in Chicago by Louis Sullivan and the younger architects – Frank Lloyd Wright, George Grant Elmslie and George Washington Maher – who trained in his office. The great Chicago fire of 1871 had destroyed nearly 20,000 buildings, yet the city managed to rebuild itself with astonishing speed. As the British novelist Wilkie Collins observed on a visit in 1874: '. . . everybody I meet uses the same form of greeting. "Two years ago, Mr Collins, this place was a heap of ruins – are you not astonished when you see it now?"' Louis Sullivan had studied and worked in Boston, Philadelphia and Paris before settling in Chicago in 1881 and joining Dankmar Adler in a partnership that lasted until 1895. He designed numerous

public buildings and offices in Chicago, including the Stock Exchange and the Carson Pirie Scott department store. He wanted his buildings to be completely free of historicism, and created broad, simple forms, based on the low flat skylines of the prairie, enlivened by rich and complex ornament abstracted from local grasses, seeds and plants.

The Scots-born George Grant Elmslie, who worked for twenty years from 1889 as Sullivan's chief draughtsman, and executed most of his ornamental designs, was possibly responsible for much of his domestic work. Elmslie designed furniture that combined geometric forms with stylized carving, as well as metalwork, leaded glass, rugs and even, for his own house, embroidered tablecovers. Like Sullivan, he believed in an 'organic' use of decorative motifs, applying a theme as simply or elaborately as required throughout a building. In 1909, when Frank Lloyd Wright left for Europe, Elmslie set up his own practice, Purcell, Feick and Elmslie, and designed many houses in the Prairie style.

George Washington Maher was equally interested in the complete interior and designed many of the furnishings for the houses he built. Beginning to work on his

Interior of the Edna Purcell residence, Minneapolis, Minnesota, designed in 1913 by George Grant Elmslie

bined the selected stylized form, which might be a lion or floral motif such as the hollyhock, honeysuckle or lotus, with a specific geometric shape. The motif – perhaps a thistle combined with an octagon, or a poppy with a straight line – was then repeated 'rhythmically' inside and out to create a sense of visual unity.

Frank Lloyd Wright, however, went beyond Sullivan or Maher's ornament abstracted from nature to make the very structure of his houses organic, to make 'aesthetic and structure completely one'. Architectural beauty, Wright believed, was the product of simple and harmonious elements clearly stated, and was derived from the economy which results from following natural laws. 'Bring out the nature of the materials,' he wrote, 'let this nature intimately into your scheme.' Style could not be imposed on a building, but grew out of the basic plan and the choice of building materials, as well as the building's position within the landscape.

Wright's interest in the relationship between nature and geometry went back to his childhood, when he had played with the Froebel blocks he later gave to his own children, and was reinforced by his interest in Japanese design, which, he felt, evoked the universal principle without losing the power of individuality. In his autobiography, Wright wrote in 1932 that 'pure design is abstraction of nature-elements in purely geometric terms', and went on to say that architecture was akin to music, that creating a building was like writing a symphony. 'When I build I often hear Beethoven's music and, yes, when Beethoven made his music I am sure he sometimes saw buildings

own account in 1888, he visited Europe twice during the 1890s, and his later work shows the influence of Voysey. Maher developed his own method of unifying the exterior and interior of a house with its furnishings through decorative details, which he called his 'motif rhythm theory'. The choice of motif should, he felt, be derived principally from the needs and temperament of the client, but he then com-

like mine in character, whatever form that may have taken then.'

In California, too, the Arts and Crafts movement provided the inspiration for the development of a distinctive local style. The 'golden state' contained not only a generous climate and a varied and beautiful landscape, from the arroyo canyons to the orange groves, but a rich and romantic mix of cultures. The American immigrant population searching for a fresh architectural and decorative style could draw not only upon their own backgrounds but also upon the adobe buildings of Mexico, the Franciscan missions from the Spanish colonial past, and the artefacts of the indigenous Indian culture.

In San Francisco, after the earthquake and fire of 1906, Arthur F. Mathews and his wife Lucia founded the Philopolis Press and the Furniture Shop with the ideal of rebuilding the city afresh. Mathews, an architect and painter who had been director of the California School of Design, had trained as a painter in Paris, and his work combined figures from the classical traditions of Europe with landscapes that were purely Californian. In the furniture and complete interiors, both private and public, that he and his wife created for the Furniture Shop, the colours, landscape and flowers of California dominate. Lucia Mathews's two great interests were horticulture and painting, and the carved, incised, inlaid, gilded and painted furniture she designed, ranging from candlesticks and picture frames to large cupboards and screens, could not be more different from the plain, backwoods style of the eastern seaboard.

Bernard Maybeck was born in New York, the son of an immigrant German wood-carver. The simple wooden chalets and bungalows he built in the Berkeley Hills and the Bay area inspired his friend and patron Charles Keeler to dedicate his book *The Simple Home* to him. To Keeler, who believed in a mystical communion with the landscape, Maybeck's homes upheld the ideal of a simple and hospitable home-life promulgated by Stickley and others, and were admirably suited to their locality.

Further south, Irving John Gill, who worked in San Diego and later in Los Angeles, built houses with the massive walls and shady arcades of the Mission style. As became an architect who had worked in Sullivan's office in Chicago in the early 1890s, he used modern materials – concrete instead of adobe – as well as natural local materials such as river boulders or redwood.

It was in Pasadena, however, that the most deeply Arts-and-Crafts-inspired houses were built – the airy wooden houses of the brothers Charles Sumner and Henry Mather Greene. Ashbee met Greene and Greene in 1909 and wrote of Charles: 'Like Lloyd Wright the spell of Japan is upon him, he feels the beauty and makes magic out of the horizontal line, but there is in his work more tenderness, more subtlety, more self-effacement than in Wright's work. It is more refined and has more repose . . . perhaps it is California that speaks rather than Illinois. . . .'

Like Wright, Greene and Greene were interested in the relationship of their houses to their settings, and this interest was expressed in their choice of local materials such as arroyo stone for foundations, paths, steps and retaining walls and wood for the houses themselves – in the Gamble House (1907–9), for example, wooden porches and stone terraces link the exterior and interior. Greene and Greene's best-known houses are low-built, with dominant gabled roofs and widely overhanging eaves that seem to secure the buildings to the ground, and the brothers combined a wide variety of influences in their style of building, ranging from Maybeck's shingled Swiss chalet houses, or Craftsman bungalows, to ornamental details and surface treatments adapted from Japanese temples and palaces. In the garden of the Cordelia A. Culbertson House, built in Pasadena in 1911, for example, a loggia, a vine-covered pergola and an Italianate water garden inspired by Edith Wharton's *Italian Villas and Their Gardens* are combined with the Japanese motif of a curving path of stepping-stones leading to a gabled oriental gate.

Despite the huge differences between the newly-settled hills of Pasadena, or the vast plains of Illinois, and leafy, rural England, architects in Britain and America were aware of one another's work and felt that they shared common concerns and interests – in materials, gardens, and the expression of harmony within the local landscape. The English climate was suited to neither the horizontal forms of the Prairie School nor the shady bungalows of California, yet there are many points of contact between Wright, Greene and Greene, Webb and Lutyens. The partnership which produced the most quintessentially English country houses was that between the young Edwin Lutyens and the middle-aged Gertrude Jekyll. As a boy, 'Ned' Lutyens had been kept at home because of his delicate health, but the illustrator Randolph Caldecott, a neighbour, had encouraged him to draw, and he went to Kensington School of Art before spending a year as a paying apprentice in the architectural office of Ernest George and Peto. A commission from a family friend in 1889 enabled him to set up in practice for himself, aged only twenty. That year, he met Miss Jekyll, introduced by a friend in the hope that she would commission him to design the house she was planning to set amidst her garden at Munstead Wood. She did, and it marked the beginning of a long and fruitful collaboration.

Lutyens absorbed much from Miss Jekyll's collection of old English furniture, and his early designs for furniture are based on Stuart and William and Mary originals. He also learnt from the photographs she took to record local life and vernacular achitecture; this record (subsequently published in 1904 as *Old West Surrey*) undoubtedly reinforced the influence of Philip Webb and Norman Shaw in the evolution of Lutyens's early 'Surrey' style. And Miss Jekyll won him several vital early commissions at the turn of the century, such as that from Edward Hudson, proprietor of *Country Life*, to build Deanery Gardens for him in Berkshire. *Country Life* went on to feature much of Lutyens's work as well as that of Miss Jekyll.

Among the other masterpieces created by Lutyens and Jekyll are Folly Farm in Berkshire, Ammerdown and Hestercombe in Somerset, and Marsh Court in Hampshire. Lutyens's 'Surrey' style combined local building techniques and materials, such as

Above: Presentation drawing by Bernard Maybeck for a townhouse for a San Francisco department store owner, 1909

half-timbering and decorative brick- and tile-work, with picturesque silhouettes of gables and ornate, seventeenth-century-style chimneys which arise out of the gardens designed and planted by Miss Jekyll. Lutyens built balconies, buttresses and walkways which, as at Folly Farm, join the gardens to the house. Gertrude Jekyll taught Lutyens not only how to make garden and house seem almost to intermingle, but also how to use the garden to link a house to its site.

Although Lutyens designed a great deal of furniture, he seldom undertook complete interiors: he had a strong sense of the way houses are naturally altered over time, and his notion of the 'organic' interior contained a powerful awareness of history. He probably felt that the furnishings best suited to his houses were antiques.

Despite his success as a country house architect, and as a creator of modern castles, such as the massive, granite Castle Drogo overlooking Dartmoor in Devon, his tastes

Overleaf: The entrance front of Gertrude Jekyll's house Munstead Wood, Munstead, Surrey, designed for her by Edwin Lutyens and completed in 1897

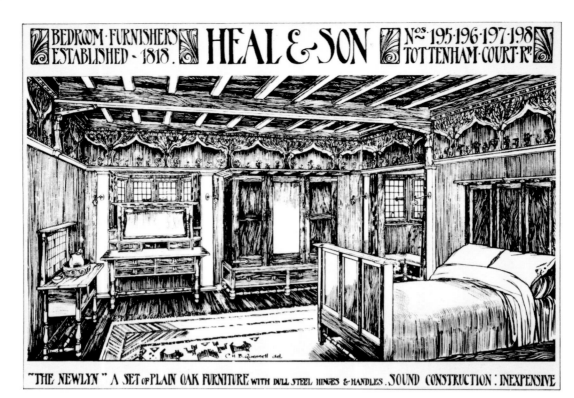

BEDROOM·FURNISHERS ESTABLISHED·1818. HEAL & SON N.ºˢ·195·196·197·198 TOTTENHAM·COURT·R.ᵈ

"THE NEWLYN" A SET ᴏꜰ PLAIN OAK FURNITURE ᴡɪᴛʜ ᴅᴜʟʟ ꜱᴛᴇᴇʟ ʜɪɴɢᴇꜱ & ʜᴀɴᴅʟᴇꜱ SOUND CONSTRUCTION : INEXPENSIVE

The Newlyn Suite, one of Ambrose Heal's earliest sets of oak furniture, illustrated in a woodcut by C.H.B. Quennell in 1898

began to veer more towards the Palladian. In 1912 he was appointed architect to the new city of Delhi, confirming his classical leanings. Later commissions included the Roman Catholic cathedral in Liverpool.

For those who could not afford to commission an architect-designed interior, there was a successor to Liberty and Co. that provided the complete English rural vernacular look: Heal and Sons. Heal's was a long-established supplier of beds and bedding, which had opened a new department for sitting-room furniture in the 1880s. Ambrose Heal, the great-grandson of the shop's founder, began to design furniture in the 'Cotswold' style established by Gimson and the Barnsleys, and his first pieces appeared in the windows of the Tottenham Court Road store in 1896. Two years later he published a catalogue of his own designs entitled *Plain Oak Furniture*, which was praised by Gleeson White in *The Studio*. The following year he published *Simple Bedroom Furniture*, a

collection of plain, homely bedroom suites that were cheap and stylish. They were exhibited in 1899 at the Arts and Crafts Exhibition Society, which Ambrose Heal joined himself in 1906, and were to prove a great commercial success.

The simple 'Newlyn' bedroom suite (all his ranges were named after such English seaside towns as Newlyn or St Ives), in fumed oak with steel handles and hinges, was illustrated in the catalogue by a distinctive woodcut of an imaginary room with low rafters, quaint leaded bay windows and an Arts and Crafts frieze around the cornice. Some of his early designs incorporated mottoes and quotations inlaid in pewter and ebony; for instance, the 'Fine Feathers' suite, in his *Plain Oak Furniture* catalogue, had inset on the wardrobe 'Fine feathers make fine birds' and on the dressing-table 'If this be vanity who'd be wise'. In 1900 Ambrose Heal took over the direction of all of Heal's advertising, using his distinctive

Oak dressing table designed
by Ambrose Heal

Arts and Crafts typography and calligraphy: by 1905, when he became managing director, he had stamped his personality on the entire store.

From 1905 Heal's sold a wide range of reasonably priced plain oak 'cottage furniture' for 'Metro-Land' dwellers, as well as cheaper, machine-made furnishings which were considered 'excellent for servants' bedrooms', and also fabrics from all the leading designers and manufacturers. Later Heal's introduced other English woods, including walnut, elm, cherry and chestnut, using light staining to enhance the grain. Dressers and dining suites were enlived with ebonized banding and with the distinctive ebony and pewter check inlay that Heal used from around 1900. In the early 1920s they introduced their 'weathered' oak finish: the grain was opened with a wire brush and the wood coated with plaster of Paris, then sanded so as to leave some plaster in the grain. The oak was finished with wax and button polish to make it easy to maintain. Heal's retained its reputation as the stylish furniture store for the middle-class intelligentsia until the 1960s, and no doubt furnished many a suburban villa in the 'mild Home County acres' celebrated so nostalgically in the poetry of the late Poet Laureate, John Betjeman, and reached by the Metropolitan Line, the first steam underground in the world:

> Lured by the lush brochure,
> Down by-ways beckoned,
> To build at last
> The cottage of our dreams.
> City clerk turns countryman again,
> And linked to the metropolis by train.
> Metro-Land.

FRANK LLOYD WRIGHT

Frank Lloyd Wright (1867-1959) was born in Wisconsin, where he studied engineering. He worked briefly for the Chicago architect J. L. Silsbee, in whose offices he met Elmslie and Maher, and in 1888 entered the offices of Adler and Sullivan, where he quickly became chief draughtsman, responsible for many of the practice's smaller domestic commissions. In 1893 he established his own practice in Oak Park, to which many young architects came to work and study, and by 1900 he had designed over fifty houses.

Wright collected Japanese prints, and was strongly influenced by Japanese arts: he visited Japan in 1905. In 1897 he was a founding member of the Chicago Society of Arts and Crafts at Hull House, and in 1900 met C. R. Ashbee, who was at that time visiting Chicago. They remained friends for years, despite their fierce arguments over the role of the machine. While Ashbee passionately supported hand-craftsmanship, with the result that only the wealthy could afford his products, Wright strongly supported the use of new technology, realizing that the use of the machine would make it possible that 'the poor as well as the rich may enjoy today beautiful surface treatments of clean strong forms'.

His early work was also influenced by Norman Shaw's revivalist style, interpreted in America by H. H. Richardson in Boston, and by the New England Shingle style, but the house which he built for himself in Oak Park in 1899 began to show his architectural philosophy, and also contained his first designs for furniture.

Between 1901 and 1909 he developed a geometric abstraction of nature, reflecting the open, quiet skylines of the prairie in low, flat houses with overhanging roofs and prominent chimneys that conveyed a traditional image of shelter. His belief in the total integration of site, structure and furnishings was manifested, for example, in the Susan Lawrence Dana House of 1902–4, for which he designed leaded glass, lighting fixtures, furniture and even fountains, or the Frederick C. Robie House of 1908 which he completely furnished.

Oak extending dining table designed by Frank Lloyd Wright in 1896 for the William C. Fricke House, Chicago. Victoria & Albert Museum, London

Influenced by the ideas of Otto Wagner in Vienna, Wright believed that the building begins with the interior space. He created open living-spaces, often with simple, built-in furniture which was a natural extension of the structure. The furnishings had also to accentuate the symbolic meaning of the house. The fireplace, the heart of the house, was often made a focal point – not just by Wright, but by many Arts and Crafts designers – as was the dining-room, where the family and guests gathered to break bread. Wright believed that 'the horizontal line is the line of domesticity', and in the Robie House the strong horizontal and vertical rhythm of the dining table and chairs is reinforced by the low ceiling and its horizontal beams.

In 1909 Wright left Chicago for Europe with the wife of a former client. On his return to America two years later, he built a new house and studio, Taliesin, in Wisconsin, but his architecture, in Chicago, California and Japan, remained somewhat static until the 1930s, when he began to work in a more Modernist style. His later buildings, such as Fallingwater, in Pennsylvania, or the Guggenheim Museum in New York, built in the late 1950s, are as coherent and strong as his early Prairie School houses.

Oak spindle chair by
Frank Lloyd Wright,
c.1908, one of several
variations of high-backed
dining chairs that he
designed

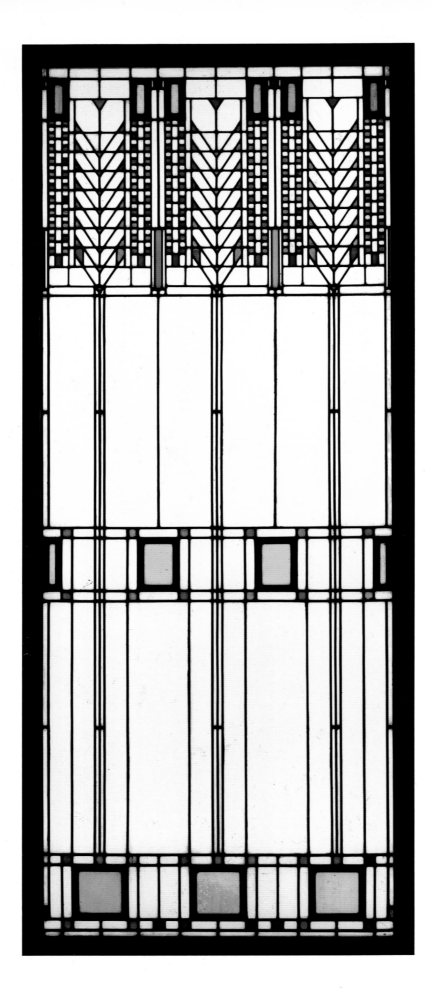

Leaded and stained glass
'Tree of Life' window
designed by Frank Lloyd
Wright for the Darwin D.
Martin House, Buffalo,
New York in 1904

Opposite: Inlaid walnut and
ebony armchair, designed
by Charles and Henry
Greene for the Blacker
House, Pasadena, *c.*1907

GREENE AND GREENE

The Gamble House, Pasadena, designed by Charles and Henry Greene, 1907–8, for one of the partners in the soap firm Proctor and Gamble and (*opposite*) a wall sconce of Honduras mahogany, ebony and leaded glass

Charles Sumner (1868–1957) and Henry Mather (1870–1954) Greene were born in Cincinnati. Charles wanted to be a painter, but both brothers studied at the Massachusetts Institute of Technology and then worked in Boston for different architectural firms. They moved to Pasadena, where their parents had just settled, in 1894.

During the 1890s they worked in a variety of styles, including Mission, New England Shingle, and colonial Queen Anne and Dutch revival. They began to be interested in Japanese design after seeing examples of Japanese architecture at the World's Columbian Exposition in Chicago in 1893, and four years later were able to enlarge their understanding of Japanese arts after meeting John Bentz, an importer of oriental antiquities and books.

In 1901 Charles Greene visited England on his honeymoon, and on his return, when *The Craftsman* began publication, he took to studying Arts and Crafts ideas, in particular the Craftsman plans for inexpensive bungalows, which had much in harmony with the Japanese architecture that he and Henry admired. In 1902 the Greenes used Stickley furniture in the James Culbertson House. Their own work was later regularly featured in *The Craftsman*.

The Robert R. Blacker House of 1907, a large, asymmetrical wooden structure set in a six-acre Japanese-style garden, was built in Pasadena for a retired lumberman. Both the house and the furniture they designed for it were influenced by Japanese design. In the David B. Gamble House in Pasadena and the Charles M. Pratt House in the Ojai Valley, they were given a free hand by the clients, both of whom were friends of the Blackers. The two houses were winter retreats, and Greene and Greene were able to oversee every detail, from the gardens to fireplace tools, abstract rugs, leaded glass and lighting fixtures such as wooden lanterns. The furniture, some of it inlaid with stylized motifs in fruitwoods, ebony or precious stones, showed great simplicity of line and form and made decorative use of pegging and dowelling or mortise-and-tenon joinery. It was Charles Greene who designed most of the furniture, which was made by two Swedish craftsmen, John and Peter Hall.

In 1916 Charles moved north to Carmel, California, where he undertook little new work. The brothers' last collaboration was in 1923.

GARDEN DESIGN

In his influential books, *The Wild Garden*, 1871, and *The English Flower Garden*, 1883, William Robinson put into words the new feeling for natural gardens. Rejecting the mid-Victorian practice of the seasonal bedding-out of annuals in strict geometric patterns, he passionately advocated wild, romantic gardens, with sweeping lawns, wide herbaceous borders and walls covered with trailing flowers that would reflect the changing seasons.

Interest in 'old-fashioned' gardens and particularly in the propagation of 'those dear old flowers', as Mrs M. J. Loftie described them – hollyhock, tiger-lily, poppy, sunflower, roses, lavender, lupin, pinks, phlox, iris, delphinium – had been growing for some time. All the Pre-Raphaelite painters had old-fashioned gardens and, at Morris's Red House, there were topiary hedges, grass walks, wattled trellises for roses and carefully preserved orchard trees. Such a style was also perfect for small suburban gardens: in 1883 the Natural History and Gardening Society at Bedford Park, for example, declared its interest in the 'cultivation of simple and old-fashioned flowers'.

Painters, architects, writers, all turned their attention to the garden, especially to the more formal topiary, clipped hedges, trellises and box edging of Italian or so-called 'Queen Anne' gardens. In 1880 E. W. Godwin and Maurice Adams published *Artistic Conservatories*, with designs for floral porches, aviaries and verandahs. In 1891 J. D. Sedding brought out *Garden Crafts Old and New*; this was followed the next year by Reginald Blomfield's *The Formal Garden in England*; in America in 1904 the novelist Edith Wharton contributed *Italian Villas and Their Gardens*; and in 1907 George Samuel Elgood, an English watercolourist who specialized in painting gardens, and who had illustrated *Some English Gardens* in 1904 for Gertrude Jekyll, published *Italian Gardens*.

Helen Allingham, an artist famous for her watercolours of cottage gardens, added *Happy England* to the genre in 1903. She was married to the Irish poet, William Allingham, and was a friend of Ruskin, Browning and Tennyson, whose garden she painted.

William Robinson, however, disagreed violently and publicly with Blomfield's ideas, most specifically over the proper use of terraces to link house and garden, and it was left to the formidable partnership of Gertrude Jekyll and Edwin Lutyens to reconcile the two approaches.

When they met in May 1889 at the house of a rhododendron collector, Miss Jekyll was forty-five and Ned Lutyens just twenty. She was being forced by increasing myopia to abandon her embroidery, silver repoussé work and wood-carving, and was increasingly concerned with the garden she was creating on her fifteen-acre plot of land next door to her mother's house in Munstead, Surrey.

She had developed an interest in gardens after reading Robinson's book and subscribing to his journal, *The Garden*, and they had met and become friends in 1875. With Lutyens, she now put her skills to professional use and by 1910 they had collaborated on nearly sixty gardens.

Getrude Jekyll was a practical gardener, supplying plants and deciding on colour harmonies, for she believed in a creative relationship with nature, using flowers and plants as an artist does the colours on his palette. She was also responsible for introducing many Japanese plants and shrubs, such as azaleas, lilies and flowering cherries, to English gardens. While she contributed the detailed planting and inspired the rose-covered pergolas, pools, steps, clipped yew, and colourful drifts of flowers that became the trademarks of their style, Lutyens decided on the formal geometry, creating paths, vistas and juxtapositions of brick, stone, water and greenery, and also designed garden seats, fountains and other features.

After 1910, Getrude Jekyll worked alone on hundreds of garden schemes while Lutyens was occupied with his more grandiose architectural plans, although they collaborated on the design of war cemeteries after the First World War. She was a regular contributor to *Country Life* and wrote many books, of which her best loved were *Wood and Garden*, 1899, and *Home and Garden*, 1900. Her influence on English gardens is almost as strong now as it was ninety years ago.

SUNDIAL IN A SCOTCH GARDEN

Above: Illustration from Reginald Blomfield's *The Formal Garden in England*, 1892

Left: A Mediterranean Garden by George Samuel Elgood, *c.*1900. Christopher Wood Gallery, London

Previous page: The garden at Hestercombe, Somerset, designed by Edwin Lutyens in 1903 and planted by Gertrude Jekyll

Part Five

THE
CONTINUING
INFLUENCE
OF THE
MOVEMENT

The Modern Movement is Born

As Europe moved closer and closer to the First World War, the debate about the true nature of good design was extended not only by new art movements, such as Cubism, De Stijl or Futurism, but by the emotive power of technological advance. By 1919 the emotional imperative to build for peace, to transform the tanks, guns and aircraft developed during the war into a technology to be used for the good of the working men who had fought alongside the artists, architects and designers in the trenches had become an urgent desire to create a new and better society. All over Europe, the arguments about the use of the machine, the role of the artist or the relevance of ornament were picked up where they had been left off in 1914.

In Italy, the Futurists, and in Holland, the founders of *De Stijl* magazine – Piet Mondrian, J. J. P. Oud and its editor Theo van Doesburg – had already demanded a style dictated by modern materials and based on the technological 'spirit of the times'. Already in pre-war Vienna, the radical architect, designer and writer Adolf Loos had condemned the decorative products of the Wiener Werkstätte as degenerate and pretentious, insisting that beauty lay not in ornament but in form. His own post-war furniture designs were plain and functional, showing an understanding of the relationship between materials and form, and his buildings were totally devoid of ornament. Although Loos admired the work of English Arts and Crafts designers, he had also responded to the methods of mass-production he had seen in America, where he had studied architecture, and he advocated mass-produced and inexpensive designs such as Thonet's bentwood chairs. The simplicity of Morris's 'Sussex' chair had triumphed, but the championship of the way of life of the craft workshop no longer seemed relevant.

In post-revolutionary Russia, the artists who had embraced abstraction joined the Vkhutemas, the reorganized Moscow art schools, and went on to develop Constructivism, which supported an exploration of form as dictated by the properties of specific materials. In 1921 they announced their alliegance to Productivism, a doctrine that held that art should be practised as a trade and that the production of well-designed articles for everyday use was of far greater value than individual expression.

In France, the Swiss architect who styled himself Le Corbusier was evolving the idea that furnishings should, like fountain pens,

The dining room in a house designed by Alvar Aalto in 1938. The evolution of such spacious and practical 'open-plan' living set the style for the 'Contemporary' look of the 1950s

telephones or office furniture, be designed as 'equipment' that would work well and fulfil the demands put upon it with the same precision that we expect from such other modern 'tools' as cars or locomotives. In Berlin in 1922, Peter Behrens, in whose studio had worked Le Corbusier, Walter Gropius and Mies van der Rohe, became artistic director of AEG. This was the first industrial company to appoint a designer to oversee the creation of a coherent corporate image, and Behrens designed not only their products – including fans, kettles, telephones and street lights – but also their buildings and their advertising and other graphics.

The designer, said these diverse founders of the Modern Movement, should become as anonymous as the engineer: the individual expression of the artist had become an irrelevance; even, said some, easel-painting itself should be reduced to a 'science' of form and colour. Mass production was the means by which a greater number of people could be supplied with good, inexpensive furnishings and everyday utensils. Architecture and design were, at last, freed totally from historicism by their relationship to such new materials as concrete, plate glass and tubular steel.

The Bauhaus has always been held up as the creative hub of Modernism, and it is true that many of the various European movements fed directly into the school, yet when the thirty-six-year-old architect Walter Gropius was appointed director of Henri van de Velde's former Kunstgewerbeschule in Weimar in 1919, his initial aims were still rooted in the English Arts and Crafts movement. Gropius's appointment as director

had been suggested by van de Velde himself, and the Bauhaus – Gropius's new name for the school – was housed in the buildings the Belgian had designed for the school that he had established with the aim of providing designs for industrial manufacture as well as to teach manual craft skills.

In his 1919 *Manifesto* Gropius wrote: 'Let us together desire, conceive and create the new building of the future, which will combine everything – architecture *and* sculpture *and* painting – in a *single form* which will one day rise towards the heavens from the hands of a million workers as the crystalline symbol of a new and coming faith.' The whole basis of the Bauhaus training was to lie in direct workshop experience in the crafts; painting and sculpture were to be regarded in the same light as woodwork, metalwork, typography or weaving. The Bauhaus was to be a community of skilled artists committed to a collaborative effort. But Gropius, it must be remembered, had opposed Muthesius in the Deutsche Werkbund in 1914 over the issue of standardization for mass production, and had supported van de Velde who had argued for the importance of individual creative expression. 'The manner of teaching [at the Bauhaus],' explained Gropius in 1919, 'arises from the character of the workshop: organic forms developed from manual skills. Avoidance of all rigidity; priority of creativity; freedom of individuality, but strict study discipline.' Ruskin's belief in individual expression remained.

Each workshop had two 'masters', as the teaching staff were now known: the students also became 'apprentices' or 'journeymen'. One of the staff-members was the technical master who was in charge of the workshop, the other, the *Formmeister*, an artist who was responsible for *Form*, or design. Early *Formmeistern* included the painters Georg Muche and Paul Klee. All students followed the same course during their first year, gaining firsthand experience of the different workshops, before choosing the medium in which they would then specialize. This preliminary course was taught initially by the Swiss painter Johannes Itten, who, as something of a guru, combined lectures on form or colour with meditative breathing exercises and other mystical ideas.

During the first couple of years, the Bauhaus attracted many Expressionist painters as teachers, including Gerhard Marcks, Georg Muche, Paul Klee and Wassily Kandinsky, who had also taught at the Moscow Vkhutemas. The items produced in the pottery or the weaving workshop were, as Gunta Stölzl, the future head of the weaving workshop, wrote in 1931, 'poems heavy with ideas, flowery embellishment, and individual experience!' But by 1923 a change had occurred; Johannes Itten was persuaded to leave and was replaced by the self-taught Hungarian artist Lazlo Moholy-Nagy, who had participated in the 'Constructivist and Dadaist Congress' organized in Weimar the previous year by Theo van Doesburg, the editor of *De Stijl*. Van Doesburg had arrived in Weimar in 1921 and began to publish the magazine from there and to offer his own course, which, although highly critical of the Bauhaus for what he considered its self-indulgent romanticism, was attended by many Bauhaus students. 'Gradually there was a shift,' recalled Gunta Stölzl. 'We no-

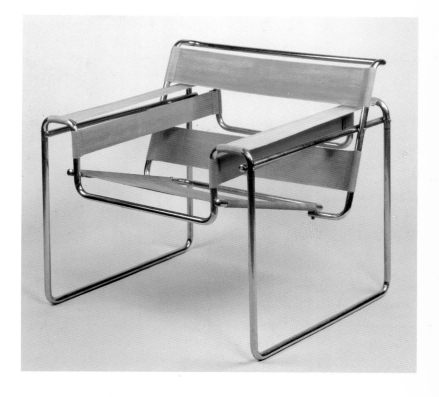

'Wassily Chair', the first tubular steel chair, designed by Marcel Breuer at the Dessau Bauhaus in 1925

ticed how pretentious these independent, single pieces were . . . the richness of colour and form . . . did not integrate, it did not subordinate itself to the home. We made an effort to become simpler, to discipline our means and to achieve a greater unity between material and function. . . . The slogan of this new era: prototypes for industry!'

It was this shift which marked the final end of the influence of the Arts and Crafts movement, and the true beginnings of Modernism. Gropius responded ably to his students' support of the new ideas expressed by van Doesburg or by Le Corbusier in *L'Esprit nouveau*, and he encouraged the *Neues Sachlichkeit* (the 'New Objectivity') backed by the new masters such as Moholy-Nagy who brought with them the Russian Constructivist doctrine – a doctrine that rejected subjective responses to art and held that it was the idea behind a work of art that mattered, that it was irrelevant whether it was executed by the hand of an artist or by a machine. In addition to his teaching of the preliminary course, Moholy-Nagy also became *Formmeister* in the metalwork shop, where students turned from jewellery and handmade silverware to the design of modern lighting or retractable shaving mirrors. From architecture to graphics, the Bauhaus championed the anonymous designer who subordinated personal expression to practical need, and who evolved, through workshop experience, prototypes for industrial mass production. Such design would contribute to the 'cathedral of socialism', hastening equality of ownership through 'worker-housing' designed and furnished by these Modernist artists. The value of the craft workshop lay not in the way of life it offered the craftsman but – as at Hoffmann's Kunstlerwerkstätte in Vienna also – in the craftsman's experience of a vital artistic

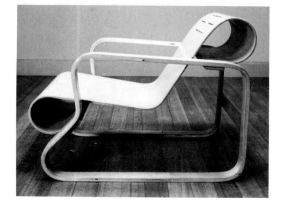

Laminated birch cantilevered armchair originally designed by Alvar Aalto for the Paimio Sanatorium, 1931–2

laboratory where new design solutions could be evolved and tested.

But the Bauhaus dream was short-lived. The defeat of the local Socialist government forced the Weimar Bauhaus to close in April 1925, and Gropius moved the school to newly-designed buildings in the industrial town of Dessau. The Dessau Bauhaus was poorly financed, and outside orders from industrial firms became a vital source of income; many of the domestic innovations we now take for granted – push-button light switches, stacking kitchen bowls or reflectors for indirect lighting – emanated from the Dessau Bauhaus.

In 1928 Gropius resigned as director of the Bauhaus and was replaced by Hannes Meyer, the former head of the architecture department. In 1930 Meyer was succeeded by Mies van der Rohe, whose tubular steel furniture had already caused a sensation at the Werkbund exhibition in Stuttgart in 1927. But in 1933 the Nazis forced the Bauhaus to close. Masters and students spread all over the world, particularly to America, where they greatly influenced generations of post-war architects and designers.

The industrial aesthetic developed at the Dessau Bauhaus, at the Moscow Vkhutemas or by Le Corbusier in Paris was by no means the only solution to the debate about the future of Arts and Crafts ideals. In Scandinavia, too, artists were encouraged to become involved with industrial production, as at the famous Swedish Orrefors glass factory, but they produced designs which remained rooted in a Ruskinian appreciation of the natural world. The Svenska Slöjdföreningen, the Swedish Society of Industrial Design, had been founded

A room in the architecture department at the Dessau Bauhaus, c.1928, with counterweighted hanging lamps designed by Marianne Brandt and Hans Przyrembel

in 1845 and in 1917 organized the Home Exhibition in Stockholm, which included twenty-three interiors, inexpensively furnished with industrially produced designs. Designers such as Carl Malmsten, who first made his name with the furniture he produced in 1916 for the new Stockholm City Hall, continued to work within the tradition of the individual workshop, using craft skills to create simplified versions of Gustavian forms, though he also produced prototypes for industrial manufacture. Bruno Mathsson, who followed him, made simple bentwood furniture of laminated beech. And in Denmark, Kaare Klint not only made furniture in the craftsman tradition, but also designed built-in storage furniture.

But it was the Finnish architect Alvar Aalto who most fully synthesized the beliefs of the Arts and Crafts movement with the needs of the machine. In 1929, when he won a competition to build a new tuber-culosis sanatorium at Paimio, near Turku in Finland, he began to design cantilevered laminated birchwood furniture. Although at this time he met Le Corbusier in Paris, and Gropius and the De Stijl designer Gerrit Rietveld in Berlin, and did experiment with tubular metal furniture, Aalto believed that the human body should come into contact only with natural materials. His designs for chairs, tables, stools, tea trolleys and desks, which are remarkable for his attention to detail, were made from laminated birch plywood, and, where necessary, moulded to fit the human form. He set up his own firm, Artek, which also produced light fittings and textiles; when his furniture was shown in London at Fortnum and Mason's in 1933, the exhibition was visited not only by Gropius and Moholy-Nagy, but also by Voysey, who apparently praised his work. Aalto's designs thus bridged the gap between the nineteenth and the twentieth centuries.

A Continuing Legacy

By the 1920s the legacy of the Arts and Crafts movement seemed to many in England to be a joke, supported only by vegetarians wearing sandals who spent their holidays in spartan holiday camps or even 'naturist' resorts. The gabled suburban houses, with tile-hung bay windows and stained-glass panels in their front doors, that sprawled along the new arterial roads, or well-meaning church halls and municipal libraries built by architects in what passed for a decent, democratic style, seemed all that was left of William Morris's Utopian dreams of beauty and equality. But this was far from the case. The visual style of the movement may have degenerated, but many of its aims were still current and active.

From Morris's 'Anti-Scrape' to the widespread concern for the rediscovery of 'lost' craft skills, the Arts and Crafts movement was essentially preservationist. The National Footpaths Preservation Society, founded in 1887, the National Trust, founded in 1895, and the Council for the Protection of Rural England, founded in 1926, were all established by supporters of the Arts and Crafts movement. And the wider concern for the visual and social environment, the acceptance that good or bad

design affects both individuals and the quality of social life, were brought more sharply into focus by the writings and agitation of architects and designers influenced by Morris and his followers.

The last organizational outpost of the Arts and Crafts movement in Britain was the Design and Industries Association, founded in 1915 following a visit by Ambrose Heal, Harry Peach and others to the 1914 Werkbund exhibition in Cologne. The DIA, which organized exhibitions, lectures and discussions, acknowledged that it was inevitable that the future of design lay with industrial mass production, and sought to convince British designers that they must learn to coexist with the needs and limitations of the machine. But although, in ceramics or textiles, designers such as Susie Cooper or the London-based Marion Dorn, did evolve a modern British style during the 1930s, in furniture and architecture, on the other hand – apart from the steel-frame furniture produced by PEL or the laminated plywood designs made by Jack Pritchard's firm Isokon – the British never really came to appreciate the potential of a 'machine aesthetic', and, in the art schools, preparation for the needs of industry remained largely ignored. Indeed, such an eminent

Screen by Duncan Grant exhibited at the opening of the Omega Workshops, London, in July 1913, photographed in Duncan Grant's studio at Charleston, Sussex

Armchair with leather
seating by Gordon Russell,
1927–8

founder-member of the DIA as W. R. Lethaby, principal of the Central School of Arts and Crafts, considered that industrial design, while it could be shapely, strong and useful, was basically characterless and inferior to craftsmanship. 'Although a machine-made thing can never be a work of art in the proper sense,' wrote Lethaby, 'there is no reason why it should not be good in a secondary order. . . .' In 1927, when Harry Peach, maker of cane furniture and founder of Dryad Handicrafts, organized the DIA display for an exhibition in Leipzig, he created a show of country crafts. However, by the early 1930s, the somewhat genteel morality that the Arts and Crafts style had come to represent was clearly seen to be hugely out of step with European advances in design.

Nevertheless, Peach was one of those who got the DIA involved in wider issues. A champion of many causes, he was secretary of the Leicestershire Footpaths Association, a prominent member of the Folk Dancing Society, and, as a personal friend of Ramsay MacDonald, a staunch supporter of the Labour Party. In the mid-1920s he started a 'Save the Countryside' campaign, and from his work developed the Council for the Protection of Rural England. He battled against litter and also involved the DIA in setting standards for shop signs and street advertisements, making people aware of the ways in which they could passively allow their towns and villages to be polluted by bad and thoughtless design.

Ambrose Heal, who had succeeded his father as chairman of Heal's in 1913, was another early member of the DIA. From 1917 Heal's organized influential exhibitions of modern European work (in particular French and Scandinavian), and of English pottery, textiles and graphics at their Mansard Gallery. In the 1930s the store sold a wide range of modern work, from Gordon Russell's 'Cotswold' furniture to Mies van der Rohe's cantilevered tubular steel chairs.

Gordon Russell, who joined the DIA in 1920, was in many ways typical of the British compromise in attitudes to craftsmanship and the machine. He had begun designing furniture in the antique furniture repair shop set up by his father to serve the needs of the Lygon Arms Hotel, which his father owned, in the small Worcestershire town of Broadway. After the First World War, he set up independently as a designer, producing traditional turned, rush-seated chairs and plain oak furniture inspired by Gimson and the Barnsleys, as well as other pieces which could be made largely by machine. In 1929 he opened his own shop in London, but was badly affected by the Wall Street Crash. During the 1930s he regained financial security by producing the cabinets designed for Murphy radios by his brother, the architect R. D. Russell. Gordon Russell had enormous admiration for all forms of craftsmanship, from stonewalling to lettering, but, despite his clear acceptance of the machine, he always insisted on quality (whether an item was produced by hand or machine), and the style of his work remained essentially rooted in the simple, 'honest' traditions of earlier Arts and Crafts designers. The English designers were never able to convey any sense of celebration of the benefits of the machine in their work.

One of the DIA's most influential

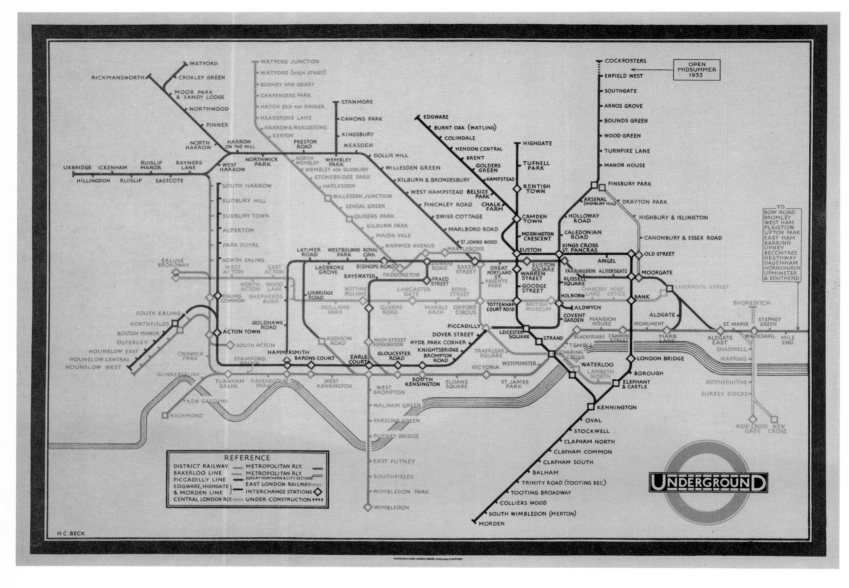

The first simplified 'Tube' map, designed for London Underground by Harry Beck in 1933. London Transport Museum

members was not a designer but an administrator, Frank Pick, who worked for the London Underground, later London Transport, and put the DIA ideals into practice, bringing art and good design to the widest possible audience. He commissioned new buildings, upholstery fabrics for trains and buses, posters, maps – the revolutionary London 'Tube' map of 1933 was the work of Harry Beck – and even a new typeface, designed in 1916 by the calligrapher Edward

Johnston, who had taught illuminating and lettering at the Central School since 1899. The London Underground posters – by a wide variety of artists – were accurately described by the Vorticist painter Wyndham Lewis as 'a people's picture gallery'.

In 1943 the aims of the DIA were further realized when Gordon Russell was made head of the Utility Design Panel, set up by the Board of Trade to specify design restrictions and create prototypes for manufacture under war-time conditions. The Utility restrictions were not entirely revoked until 1953, when it was recognized that the Utility Panel had helped to spread awareness of good mass-produced design: indeed, some Labour supporters believed that the restrictions should have been kept in force as part of a socialist plan for greater equality.

But, on the whole, the years from 1910 to 1939 were idiosyncratic and eclectic. In 1913 the art critic and painter Roger Fry had founded the Omega Workshops, with Vanessa Bell and Duncan Grant as co-directors. The purpose of the Omega, which was partly inspired by Paul Poiret's Atelier Martine in Paris, was to publicize Post-Impressionism and to give those English painters whose work was unpopular some small dependable income. The Omega barely survived the war, but it did introduce abstraction and a new, vibrant sense of colour to textiles and wall coverings. A bolder use of colour also appeared in the paintings, furniture and rugs by Frank Brangwyn, a Belgian-born painter who had worked briefly for Morris and Co. in the 1880s before setting out on adventures as a seafarer. The Indonesian textile-printing art of batik enjoyed a revival in Europe and America: the Glasgow artist Jessie M. King learnt batik in Paris before the war, and later taught the craft in Scotland, while, in America, Lydia Bush-Brown made batik popular for clothes and wallhangings.

In 1919 Robert Thompson began his career as the 'Mouseman' of Kilburn, the Yorkshire village where he was born. Thompson worked with his father, the village joiner, carpenter and wheelwright, but, inspired by the medieval carving in

Page from the 1943 Utility Furniture catalogue, illustrating a bedroom

nearby Ripon Cathedral, began carving in wood. In 1919 he received his first commission from Ampleforth, a Catholic boys' school, and went on to work for many other colleges and churches, including York Minster, and also hotels; by the 1930s he employed thirty men. He worked only in English oak, and his furniture is distinguished not only by the small carved mouse that always appears somewhere on each piece, but also by the characteristic rippled surface achieved by the use of an adze, an ancient tool the use of which he revived. Thompson died in 1955, but his Kilburn workshop continues to produce his designs, and several of those who worked for him have set up their own workshops locally, 'signing' their pieces with a carved squirrel, eagle, fox or beaver.

The one aspect of the Arts and Crafts movement which found distinctive

abcdefghjkmopqrstuvx
abcdefghjkmopqrstuvxyz
ABDEGHJKMNQRSTV

The *Gill Sans* typeface designed by Eric Gill for the Monotype Corporation, 1927–8

expression in the inter-war years in England was the ideal of the 'Simple Life' which had already been formulated in different ways by William Morris, Edward Carpenter and C. R. Ashbee. It was not only a return to the land, but a search for a simpler, more harmonious relationship with nature, with work and with other people. Those who espoused the Simple Life, for instance Eric Gill or Ethel Mairet, supported a return to humanity's intimate association with the artefacts which surround daily life, and a notion of human value acquired and practised through workshop experience. Most of the new generation of craftspeople worked independently, but they met to discuss their philosophies and to share notes on ways of selling their work. A network of guilds and galleries emerged, virtually all founded and run by women, including the Red Rose Guild in Manchester, the Three Shields Gallery and the Little Gallery in London, the Sussex-based Guild of Weavers, Spinners and Dyers, and the short-lived New Handworkers' Gallery, founded in London in 1928. The new look relied upon attention to detail, texture, a subtle colour sense and, most of all, a kind of inner integrity which expressed the almost spiritual values of the Simple Life.

The weaver Ethel Mairet spanned both generations of Arts and Crafts practitioners. She married in 1902 and accompanied her husband, Ananda Coomaraswamy, to Ceylon, where they made a study of local arts and handicrafts. On their return in 1907 they settled near Chipping Campden, where Ethel's brother, the jeweller Fred Partridge, had worked for Ashbee's Guild of Handicraft. Ashbee renovated their ancient house, Norman Chapel, and Coomaraswamy took over Ashbee's Essex House Press. But Ethel's marriage failed in 1911, she left Gloucestershire, and began to study the arts of vegetable dyeing, and weaving. In 1913 she married Philip Mairet, a young draughtsman from Ashbee's architectural office, celebrating with lunch at a vegetarian restaurant. During a troubled war (when Philip, who opposed the hostilities, first worked for the Red Cross then, when conscripted, was imprisoned for refusing to obey orders) Ethel settled in the Sussex village of Ditchling, where she set up a weaving workshop named Gospels.

Ditchling already housed a number of

craftspeople. Eric Gill had moved there in 1907 and was joined by Edward Johnston, his former tutor at the Central School, together with his family, and by Douglas Pepler, a friend from Hammersmith, who founded the Ditchling Press which published Ethel Mairet's pioneering book *Vegetable Dyes* in 1916. Gill was inspired by both medieval European and ancient Indian art, and produced typography, engraving and sculpture. In 1913 he and Pepler had founded the Guild of St Joseph and St Dominic, hoping to create a Catholic community of craftsmen and their families – a 'cell of good living' – but, as was typical of the man, Gill left the community in 1924 to start afresh in a remote Welsh valley. Nevertheless, the Ditchling community – not just the Catholic Guild of SS Joseph and Dominic but also the Johnstons, Mairets and Partridges – agreed on a rough philosophical basis founded on friendship and the feeling of common purpose that bound them together. The independent craftspeople of Ditchling, sculptor, printer, calligrapher, weaver and jeweller, provided the new generation of craftworkers with a vivid example of the Simple Life in action.

In the early 1920s a Slade School graduate, Phyllis Barron, who had begun to experiment with the difficult and largely forgotten art of discharge-printing – printing with wooden blocks on indigo-dyed cotton, then using nitric acid to discharge the colour and leave a white pattern on a blue ground – wrote to Ethel Mairet after reading *Vegetable Dyes*, and was invited to stay at Gospels for a few weeks to perfect her dyeing techniques. From 1923 Barron, as she was always known, worked in partnership with

Dorothy Larcher, who had studied textile-printing in India; the two printed their extremely sophisticated, semi-abstract designs with wooden blocks on cotton, linen, silk and wool, either by discharge indigo printing or by direct printing with natural vegetable dyes such as quercitron or madder and mineral colours such as iron and chrome. In 1930 they moved their workshop from London to Gloucestershire. Barron and Larcher remained friends with Ethel Mairet, and they frequently exhibited together at the specialist craft galleries.

Page from *The Lord's Song* by Eric Gill, 1934. Bodleian Library, Oxford

Ethel Mairet's workshop,
Gospels, in Sussex

In 1925 Barron and Larcher had been joined by a young graduate from the Royal College of Art, Enid Marx, who learned their techniques and went on to found her own fabric-printing workshop in London. Marx is an extremely versatile artist, who also specialized in wood engravings and designed book jackets, patterned papers and stamps. During the Second World War, Gordon Russell made her responsible for the design of Utility furnishing textiles. After the war, with Margery Lambert, she wrote two illustrated books on English popular and folk art.

Ethel Mairet also knew the pioneering potter Bernard Leach, who greatly admired her work. In 1928 Philip Mairet set up the New Handworkers' Gallery in London, which showed work by Leach, Michael Cardew, Barron and Larcher, Ethel Mairet and the furniture maker A. Romney Green. The Gallery also sold a series of pamphlets written by Philip Mairet, Leach, Gill and Romney Green, which expressed their beliefs in the spiritual values of their work. The pamphlets were printed at St Dominic's Press by Pepler (formerly Douglas but now, following his conversion to Catholicism, known as Hilary). The new craft ethic began with the same first principles advocated by Pugin, Webb and Morris: the architect or designer must have a thorough understanding of his or her materials. 'To make a perfect scarf,' as Ethel Mairet wrote, 'one must begin with the sheep.'

At Gospels, Ethel Mairet took paying students at her Ditchling School of Weaving: Gill's daughter Petra learned weaving there, and by the 1930s students were coming from Europe to benefit from her skills as a dyer.

During the 1930s Ethel Mairet also travelled extensively throughout Europe. In 1936 she met Alvar Aalto in Helsinki, and two years later visited Gunta Stölzl (or Frau Sharon, as the former head of the Bauhaus weaving workshop had now become) in Zurich and saw several Deutsche Werkstätten exhibitions in Germany. In 1939 she published *Hand-Weaving Today: Traditions and Changes*, in which she praised the work of the Bauhaus weaving workshop for producing prototypes for industry: 'weaving', she wrote, 'has set itself up on a pedestal as "art" . . . it must be part of a building . . . or associated with the necessities of life'. She believed that, on the model of the Bauhaus, independent craft workshops such as

Gospels could influence industrialists and so ultimately supply the consumer with better designs. Unlike her old friend Ashbee, who had seen his Guild as being in direct competition with manufacturers, Ethel Mairet saw that her own work (firmly rooted as it was in the values of the Simple Life) and the craft workshop's ability to produce work of excellent quality and technical innovation could perfectly complement the needs of the industrial manufacturer. The craft workshop was thus of both spiritual and practical relevance to the commercial world, and some of those who studied with Ethel Mairet, such as Marianne Straub, went on to apply their experience successfully within the context of industry, as did craftworkers also in Europe and America.

The work of this inter-war generation of craftspeople freed itself totally from historical borrowings (which were seen as providing only a 'false unity'), yet it retained and strengthened the essential Arts and Crafts belief in the supremacy of the materials, in the vital importance of personal expression through hand-work, and in the role of such work within the life of the individual and society. Ethel Mairet, Bernard Leach, Enid Marx and the numerous other potters, printers, puppet-makers, weavers or calligraphers who were their friends and associates, influenced those craftspeople who sought their own form of the Simple Life during the 1960s and who went on to found the Crafts Council to champion both the preservation of traditional craft skills and the work of the artist-craftsman. Many people who do not themselves practise craft skills continue to fight today to support the ideals of the Simple Life through environmentalism, animal welfare and other 'green' issues. The challenge that the original adherents of the Arts and Crafts movement posed to the blanket of industrialization that threatened to swamp the values they held dear remains as valid as ever.

'Butterfly', positive block-prints in iron on coarse cotton by Phyllis Barron and Dorothy Larcher

BRITISH ARTIST-POTTERS

From left to right: Stoneware cup with ashglaze made in Ajuba, Nigeria, in the late 1950s, and an earthenware bowl, slipware, made in Winchcombe, Gloucestershire *c.*1928–9, both by Michael Cardew; a stoneware vase with ash-glaze made by Katharine Pleydell Bouverie at Kilmington in 1960; a stoneware vase with Hakeme glaze with iron brushwork by Shoji Hamada, 1930; and a stoneware pot with ash-glaze made by Bernard Leach at St Ives, 1960

Bernard Leach (1887–1979), who made his first pots at a *raku* party in Japan in 1911, not only revitalized lost traditions of English pottery but also, through his writings and teaching, put forward a vastly influential new philosophy of craftsmanship. Born in Hong Kong, he spent several years of his childhood in Japan and Singapore, before moving to London where he studied at the Slade School. On his return to Japan, he spent nine years studying early Japanese, Korean and Chinese pottery and learning the techniques used by traditional Japanese potters. In 1922 he returned to England accompanied by Shoji Hamada, a young Japanese potter, who helped him to build a kiln in St Ives, Cornwall, where he began to research traditional English techniques of earthenware, stoneware and slipware pottery.

Hamada returned to Japan in 1923, but during the 1920s several other potters joined Leach in St Ives – Michael Cardew, Katharine Pleydell Bouverie and Norah Braden – fulfilling his ideal of a loose community of artist-potters. Pleydell Bouverie devoted her life to researching the different wood- and vegetable-ash glazes, setting up her own kiln at her parental home, Coleshill, where she was joined by Norah Braden. She later moved to Kilmington Manor, Wiltshire, where she continued to pot until her death. She said that she never learned to handle a brush, and her pots relied on the exquisite range of colour in her ash glazes – rich cream, black, smoky blue or green, or dove grey.

Michael Cardew, who was primarily interested in earthenware and slip-glaze decoration, left St Ives in 1926 and set up his own pottery in Devon; in the 1930s he began to work in tin-glazed stoneware. The three years from 1942 were spent in Ghana, and in 1950 he returned to Africa, this time to Nigeria, where he remained for fifteen years and founded a Pottery Training Centre. In Africa, he discovered a more flamboyant sense of form and decoration, often using rich dark browns and black glazes decorated with free, vigorous brushwork.

Hamada, although he frequently visited England, continued to work in Japan, where his meditative approach to ceramics influenced a whole generation of potters.

Leach never tried to achieve uniform perfection, believing passionately that a good pot was created intuitively and should reflect the harmony between the potter and his materials, as well as his skill and artistic judgement. He expressed his views in 1940 in *A Potter's Book*: '. . . it seems reasonable to expect that beauty will emerge from a fusion of the individual character and culture of the potter with the nature of his materials – clay, pigment, glaze – and his management of the fire, and that consequently we may hope to find in good pots those innate qualities which we most admire in people. It is for this reason that I consider the mood, or nature, of a pot to be of first importance. . . . No process of reasoning can be a substitute for or widen the range of our intuitive knowledge. . . .' Leach continued to make pots until his eyesight failed in the 1970s.

Bibliography

AGIUS, PAULINE, *British Furniture 1880–1915*, Woodbridge, Suffolk, The Antique Collectors' Club, 1978

ANSCOMBE, ISABELLE, *A Woman's Touch: Women in Design from 1860 to the Present Day*, London, Virago, 1984

—— and GERE, CHARLOTTE, *Arts and Crafts in Britain and America*, London, Academy Editions, 1978

Arts and Crafts Essays, by members of the Arts and Crafts Exhibition Society, London, Longmans Green & Co, 1893

ASHBEE, C. R., *Craftsmanship in Competitive Industry*, Campden, Gloucestershire, Essex House Press, 1908

—— *Modern English Silverwork*, Campden, Gloucestershire, Essex House Press, 1909

ASLIN, ELIZABETH, *E. W. Godwin: Furniture and Interior Decoration*, London, John Murray, 1986

BARRETT, HELENA and PHILLIPS, JOHN, *Suburban Style: The British Home 1840–1960*, London, Macdonald Orbis, 1987

BILLCLIFFE, ROGER, *Charles Rennie Mackintosh: The Complete Furniture, Furniture Drawings and Interior Designs*, Guildford and London, John Murray, 1979

BORISOVA, HÉLÈNE and STERNINE, GREGORY, *Art Nouveau Russe*, Paris, Editions de Regard, 1987.

BROWN, JANE, *Gardens of a Golden Afternoon, the Story of a Partnership: Edwin Lutyens and Gertrude Jekyll*, London, Allen Lane, 1982

CATHER, DAVID M., *Furniture of the American Arts and Crafts Movement*, New York, New American Library, 1981

CLARK, GARTH and HUGHTO, MARGIE, *A Century of Ceramics in the United States, 1878–1978*, New York, E. P. Dutton, 1979

COOK, E. T. and WEDDERBURN, A. (ed.) *The Complete Works of John Ruskin*, 39 vols., London, George Allan, 1903–12.

COMINO, MARY, *Gimson and the Barnsleys*, London, Evans Brothers, 1980

COOPER, JEREMY, *Victorian and Edwardian Furniture and Interiors: from the Gothic Revival to Art Nouveau*, London, Thames & Hudson, 1987

CRANE, WALTER, *An Artist's Reminiscences*, London, Methuen, 1907

CRAWFORD, ALAN, *C. R. Ashbee: Architect, Designer and Romantic Socialist*, New Haven and London, Yale University Press, 1985

CROOK, J. MORDAUNT, *William Burges and the High Victorian Dream*, New Haven and London, John Murray, 1981

DUNCAN, ALASTAIR, *Art Nouveau and Art Deco Lighting*, London, Thames & Hudson, 1978

GAUNT, WILLIAM and CLAYTON-STAMM, M.D.E., *William de Morgan*, London, Studio Vista, 1971

GERE, CHARLOTTE and MUNN, GEOFFREY C., *Artists' Jewellery: Pre-Raphaelite to Arts and Crafts*, Woodbridge, Suffolk, Antique Collectors' Club, 1989

GIROUARD, MARK, *Sweetness and Light: the 'Queen Anne' Movement 1860–1900*, Oxford, Oxford University Press, 1977

GODDEN, SUSANNA, *At The Sign of The Four Poster: A History of Heal's*, London, Heal & Son Ltd, 1984

HANKS, DAVID A., *The Decorative Designs of Frank Lloyd Wright*, New York, E. P. Dutton, 1979

HARRISON, MARTIN, *Victorian Stained Glass*, London, Barrie & Jenkins, 1980

HASLAM, MALCOLM, *English Art Pottery 1865–1915*, Woodbridge, Suffolk, Antique Collectors' Club, 1975

—— *The Martin Brothers, Potters*, London, Richard Dennis, 1978.

HAWEIS, Mrs H. R. (MARY ELIZA), *The Art of Decoration*, London, Chatto & Windus, 1881

—— *Beautiful Houses*, London, Sampson Low & Co, 1882

HENDERSON, PHILIP, *William Morris, his Life, Work and Friends*, London, Thames & Hudson, 1967

HESKETT, JOHN, *Design in Germany 1870–1918*, London, Trefoil Design Library, 1986

HOWARTH, THOMAS, *Charles Rennie Mackintosh and the Modern Movement*, London, Routledge & Kegan Paul, 1977

IRVINE, LOUISE, *Doulton in the Nursery*, Vol. 3 in Royal Doulton Series Ware, London, Richard Dennis, 1986

JEKYLL, FRANCIS, *Gertrude Jekyll: A Memoir*, London, Jonathan Cape, 1934

JEWSON, NORMAN, *By Chance I Did Rove*, Cirencester, Earle & Ludlow, 1951; reprinted Warwickshire, Roundwood Press, 1973

KIRKHAM, PAT, *Harry Peach*, London, The Design Council, 1979

KOCH, ROBERT, *Louis C. Tiffany: Rebel in Glass*, New York, Crown Publishers Inc., 1964

KORNWOLF, JAMES D., *M.H. Baillie Scott and the Arts and Crafts Movement*, Baltimore and London, The Johns Hopkins Press, 1972

LARNER, GERALD and CELIA, *The Glasgow Style*, Edinburgh, Paul Harris Publishing, 1979

LETHABY, W.R., *Philip Webb and his Work*, Oxford, Oxford University Press, 1935; reprinted London, Raven Oak Press, 1979

MACCARTHY, FIONA, *The Simple Life: C.R. Ashbee in the Cotswolds*, London, Lund Humphries, 1981

—— *Eric Gill: A Lover's Quest for Art and God*, London, E.P. Dutton, 1989

MACKAIL, J.W., *The Life of William Morris*, 2 vols., London, Longmans Green & Co, 1899

MACKMURDO, A.H., 'The History of the Arts and Crafts Movement', and 'Autobiographical Notes', unpublished typescripts, William Morris Gallery, Walthamstow, London

MORRIS, MAY (ed.), *The Collected Works of William Morris*, 24 vols., London, Longmans Green & Co, 1910–15

MUTHESIUS, HERMANN, *Das Englische Haus*, Berlin, Wasmuth, 1904–5

NAYLOR, GILLIAN, *The Arts and Crafts Movement*, London, Studio Vista, 1971

ORMOND, SUZANNE and IRVINE, MAY G., *Louisiana's Art Nouveau: The Crafts of the Newcomb Style*, Louisiana, Pelican Publishing Company, 1976

OTTEWILL, DAVID, *The Edwardian Garden*, New Haven and London, Yale University Press, 1989

PARRY, LINDA, *Textiles of the Arts and Crafts Movement*, London, Thames & Hudson, 1988

—— *Morris and Company Textiles*, London, Thames & Hudson, 1983

PECK, HERBERT, *The Book of Rookwood Pottery*, New York, Crown Publishers Inc., 1968

PEVSNER, NIKOLAUS, *Pioneers of The Modern Movement from William Morris to Walter Gropius*, London, Faber & Faber, 1936 (revised edition published as *Pioneers of Modern Design*, London, Penguin Books, 1960)

RUSSELL, GORDON, *Designer's Trade*, London, George Allen & Unwin, 1968

SCHILDT, GÖRAN, *Alvar Aalto: The Decisive Years*, New York, Rizzoli, 1986

SCHWEIGER, WERNER J., *Wiener Werkstätte: Design in Vienna 1903–1932*, London, Thames & Hudson, 1984

TILBROOK, A.J., *The Designs of Archibald Knox for Liberty and Co.*, London, Ornament Press, 1976

VAN LEMMEN, HANS, *Victorian Tiles*, Aylesbury, Bucks, Shire Publications Ltd, 1981

VOLPE, TOD M. and CATHERS, BETH, *Treasures of the American Arts and Crafts Movement 1890–1920*, London, Thames & Hudson, 1988

WEDGWOOD, A., *A.W.N. Pugin and the Pugin Family*, London, Victoria & Albert Museum, 1985

WHEELER, CANDACE, *Yesterdays in a Busy Life*, New York, Harper and Bros, 1918

WINDSOR, ALAN, *Peter Behrens, Architect and Designer*, London, The Architectural Press, 1981

WINGLER, HANS M., *The Bauhaus*, Cambridge, Mass, MIT Press, 1976

EXHIBITION CATALOGUES

Victorian Church Art, Victoria & Albert Museum, London, 1971

Christopher Dresser 1834–1904, Richard Dennis and John Jesse, The Fine Art Society, London, 1972

Mathews: Masterpieces of the California Decorative Style, Oakland Museum, California, 1972

The Arts and Crafts Movement in America 1876–1916, edited by Robert Judson Clark, Princeton University, Princeton University Press, 1972

California Design, 1910, Anderson, Moore and Winter, Pasadena Center, California, 1974

C. F. A. Voysey, Architect and Designer 1857–1941, Lund Humphries, London, 1978

A London Design Studio 1880–1963: The Silver Studio Collection, Lund Humphries, London, 1980

W. A. S. Benson 1854–1924, Haslam & Whiteway, London, 1981

Lutyens, The Work of the English Architect Sir Edwin Lutyens, 1896–1944, Arts Council of Great Britain, Hayward Gallery, London, 1981

Scandinavian Modern Design 1880–1980, edited by David R. McFadden, Cooper-Hewitt Museum, Harry N. Abrams Inc., New York 1982

Italy 1900–1945, The Mitchell Wolfson Jr. Collection of Decorative & Propaganda Arts, Miami-Dade Community College, Miami, Florida, 1984

A Decorative Art: Nineteenth-century Wallpapers, Whitworth Art Gallery, Manchester, 1985

In Pursuit of Beauty: Americans and the Aesthetic Movement, Metropolitan Museum of Art, New York, Rizzoli, 1986

'The Art that is Life': The Arts & Crafts Movement in America, 1875–1920, Wendy Caplan, Museum of Fine Arts, Boston, Mass., 1987

Art Nouveau in Munich: Masters of Jugendstil, Philadelphia Museum of Art, Philadelphia Museum of Art and Prestel Verlag, Munich, 1988

Walter Crane: Artist, Designer and Socialist, Whitworth Art Gallery, Manchester, 1989

Acknowledgements

178 upper left, 173 Annan Collection, Glasgow; 166 Arcaid/Richard Bryant; 61 left The Art Institute of Chicago. All rights reserved. Photo © 1990. Gift of Raymond W. Sheets; 59 Photo from L'Art Décoratif des Ateliers de la princesse Tenichef. Edition 'Sodrougestivo' St Petersburg 1906; 71 lower left, 75 right Courtesy Felicity Ashbee; 63, 183 left, 183 right K. Barlow Ltd., London; 2 Bateman's, Sussex. National Trust; 213 Bauhaus Archiv, Berlin. Photo Walter Peterhaus; 180 Bildarchiv des Österreichisches Nationalbibliothek; 20, 25, 31, 33, 80, 94, 113, 117, 118, 141, 204–5 Bridgeman Art Library; 48, 112, 123 © British Architectural Library/ RIBA; 115 lower left, 115 upper Cheltenham Art Gallery and Museums; 6, 34, 35, 45, 77 lower left, 81, 86, 90, 115 lower right, 119, 121, 129, 156, 175, 177, 181 left, 184 lower, 186, 195, 197, 198, 200, 211 Christie's, London; 46, 49, 77 right, 89, 133, 136, 137, 159, 199 Christie's, New York; 191 College of Environmental Design, Documents Collection, University of California; 82 Cooper-Hewitt Museum, New York Art Resource; 192–3 © Country Life; 222, 223 Courtesy Crafts Study Centre, Bath; 145 Richard Dennis; 194 Design Museum, London; 42, 44, 72, 143 Mary Evans Picture Library; 26, 41, 71 lower right, 85 right, 152, 178 lower left The Fine Art Society Ltd; 146 Fogg Art Museum, Harvard University, Cambridge, Mass. Bequest Greville L. Winthrop; 208 Fritz von Schulenberg Photography Ltd; 219 Geffrye Museum, London; 68–9, 71 upper, 73 upper, 83 right, 92–3, 134, 138–9, 225 Lark Gilmer; 154 lower left, 154 right Collection: Glasgow School of Art; 168, 214, 216 Photo © Howard Grey; 17, 30, 103, 205 right Guildhall Library; 39 Hammersmith and Fulham Archives. © Hammersmith and Fulham Public Libraries; 8 left, 52, 83 right, 144 lower, 150 left, 212 Courtesy of Haslam and Whiteway Ltd; 12, 140 Ian Jones, London. Photo courtesy of Haslam and Whiteway Ltd; 47, 85 left The Jordan-Volpe Gallery, New York; 77 upper left, The Jordan-Volpe Gallery, New York, Photo Rita McMahon, New York; 203 Andrew Lawson; 126 Courtesy Liberty, London. Photo Westminster City Archives; 218 London Transport Museum; 73 lower Manchester City Art Gallery; part openers Manx Museum and National Trust. Fabrics available from Alexander Beauchamp, Griffin Mill, Thrupp, Glos. GL5 2AZ and Christopher Hyland Inc., Suite 1714, D&D Building, 979 Third Avenue, New York, N.Y. 10022, USA; 83 left Metropolitan Museum of Art, New York. Gift of Kenneth O. Smith, 1969. Photo David Allison; 116 Metropolitan Museum of Art, New York. Gift of Sunworthy Wall Coverings, a Borden Company 1987; 61 right, 182 Munich, Stadtmuseum; 109 Museum of Finnish Architecture. Photo Granath; 111 National Museum, Stockholm. Photo Statens Konstmuseer; 106 Courtesy National Park Service, Frederick Law Olmsted National Historic Site; 98 National Trust Photographic Library; 170, 178–9 National Trust for Scotland; 95 Courtesy New York Historical Society; 15 Courtesy Friends of Olana, Inc. Photo Michael Frederick; 189 The Oakland Museum, gift of the Art Guild. Photo Joe Samberg; 8 right Phillips; 29 Philadelphia Museum of Art. Gift of Charles T. Shenkle, in memory of his mother, Mrs Edna H. Shenkle; 150 right The Principal and Fellows of Newnham College, Cambridge; 172, 181 right Sotheby's, London; 67 © 1990 Sotheby's Inc; 188 University Art Museum, Santa Barbara, California; 8, 9, 25, 28, 37, 40–41, 78, 80, 100–101, 117, 118, 124, 127, 144 upper, 184–5, 185, 196 Courtesy of the Victoria and Albert Museum; 128, 132, 135 Virginia Museum of Fine Arts. Gift of Sydney and Francis Lewis; 157 left, 157 right Photo courtesy Tod Volpe, Los Angeles, California; 163 upper Wartski Ltd, London; 161, 163 lower left, 163 lower right John Jesse, London/Wartski; 57 Whitworth Art Gallery, Manchester; 36, 55, 74, 120, 154 upper left The William Morris Gallery, Walthamstow, London.

Index

❧